Systematic
Political
Theory

Merrill Political Science Series

Under the Editorship of

John C. Wahlke

Department of Political Science
State University of New York, Stony Brook

Systematic Political Theory

Michael A. Weinstein

Purdue University

Charles E. Merrill Publishing Company
A Bell & Howell Company
Columbus, Ohio

ISBN: 0-675-09200-0

Library of Congress Catalog Card Number: 72-151749

1 2 3 4 5 6 7 8 9–76 75 74 73 72 71

Printed in the United States of America

To my students at Purdue University, who have provided an intellectual life to be envied by any scholar

Preface

This book is an attempt to treat current American theories of political behavior as serious attempts to answer important questions about political existence. This aim makes the book differ from other analyses of contemporary
political theory which try to show how well present theories measure up to
the criteria of an ideal natural science of political behavior. Whether or not it
is useful to compare political theories to an ideal scientific theory, current
American theories of political behavior pose meaningful questions about public existence, present concepts through which these questions can be tenta-
tively answered and develop imaginative perspectives on political life. Thus,
they carry on the classical tradition in political thought in a new form. In
regenerating the study of political theory in the United States one must begin
with the theories of political behavior. They are the most formidable structures in contemporary political science. In this book, such theories are classified according to the questions that they pose, and particular attention is paid
to their overall perspectives on public existence. Thus, the way is cleared for
the entry of theories of political behavior into the mainstream of political
thought.

This book is the first of several, written or projected, which will explore
contemporary political thought from the point of view of recasting its
assumptions. It marks only the first step of classification. Later efforts will
undertake historical and ontological analysis preparatory to a synthesis of
current political theories on a humanist basis.

In preparing this book several people deserve special thanks. Professor John
Wahlke of SUNY at Stony Brook gave the manuscript a careful reading and
provided many valuable suggestions for improvement. Mr. Roger Ratliff of

the Charles E. Merrill Publishing Company was a sensitive and helpful editor. Through continuous discussion, Deena Weinstein made the most profound intellectual contribution. The vigorous circle of students at Purdue University who care about the regeneration of political theory have provided an exceptional experience in theoretical interchange.

Contents

Political Theory

Political theory, as it will be treated in this book, can be viewed as an activity that involves posing questions, developing responses to those questions and creating imaginative perspectives on the public life of human beings. Like all fields of intellectual endeavor, the subject of political theory can best be understood by appreciating the questions associated with its study. There is no correct definition of the scope of political theory. The scope of an intellectual activity is created by efforts to answer the questions that are posed within it. Writers who pretend that they can fruitfully discuss the conclusions of political theorists without investigating the questions that they have posed are studying dead cultural products rather than living human activities. The great political theorists created their works in response to problems that they discovered in the realms of practical affairs or speculative thought. The best way to become a political theorist, or at least to appreciate the work of political theorists, is to become seriously concerned about a problem in public life. Efforts to resolve that problem will lead to a search for appropriate concepts through which to describe public life. Once the relationships between these concepts, and their validity, become important, one is engaged in the activity of political theory.

In the contemporary world, people pose many questions about their public lives. Examples of such questions are readily available in magazines and newspapers, on television and radio news reports, and in casual discussions about public affairs. Many people are concerned with whether or not the United States should fight wars in Southeast Asia. They ask, Should the United States have become militarily involved in Viet Nam? Most political theorists would not be satisfied with a question in this form. They would maintain that a more general question must be answered before the specific query can be seriously considered. Most political theorists would rephrase the question about American military involvement to read, When should a nation become militarily involved in another nation? If they could agree upon a set of criteria for justifying military involvement they could decide whether or not American military involvement in Viet Nam measured up to the standard. Such construction of general standards of right behavior is often called *normative theory*. The term normative is derived from the word norm, a model or standard of achievement. Normative political theorists discuss the right or correct standards in the conduct of public life. Much of the history of political theory in the West can be summed up as a series of debates among normative theorists about the nature of the political good and the possibility of knowing right standards of public conduct.

If one is concerned with American military involvement in Southeast Asia, he need not pose the questions of normative theory. Instead, he may ask, Why did the United States become militarily involved in Viet Nam? Again, most political theorists would not be satisfied with a question in this form. Before they attempted to respond to the specific question, they would try to answer a more general query. They would rephrase the question about American military involvement to read, Why does a nation become militarily involved in another nation? If they could discover a set of conditions in which military involvement occurred, they could respond to the specific question by stating: "The United States became militarily involved in Viet Nam because conditions 'a,b,c, . . . , n' were present." Such inquiry into the general conditions in which political phenomena occur is often called *empirical* or *descriptive theory*.

The theories that we will discuss in this book are primarily empirical theories of political activity. The theorists under discussion are primarily concerned with understanding why political activities are patterned in certain ways. It would be a mistake, however, to say that they completely ignore the problems of political good and right political conduct. While some of them make a sharp distinction between the statements of normative theory and empirical theory, others, like Morton Kaplan, believe that no such clear separation can be made. Further, an imaginative perspective on public affairs can be derived from the writings of all the empirical theorists, and this imaginative perspective usually implies some normative judgments.

While the theorists represented in this book are mainly empirical political theorists, they are also members of the behavioral movement in political science. Frank J. Sorauf, a student of the behavioral movement, has summarized the main features of this complex intellectual development. Sorauf points out that before World War II political science was a special case in the social sciences. It had neither the central organizing concepts of economics, the concern with individual behavior of anthropology, sociology and psychology, nor the organizing value of time and narrative of history. Political science had no clear intellectual identity: "It was a heterogeneous, plural, and diverse discipline with little agreement about its central concerns, its methods, and its basic goals."[1] After World War II, a movement that began at the University of Chicago to bring political science closer to anthropology, sociology and psychology, gained increasing support. Sorauf maintains that the behavioral movement had four basic goals for political science. First, the behavioralists wanted political scientists to explore new kinds of data: "They would bring to the study of politics a new concern for the individual and group behavior that goes on within political institutions."[2] Second, the behavioralists advocated new methods for studying political phenomena. They undertook survey research, statistical analysis and various types of disciplined field work. Third, the behavioralists wanted political scientists to use new concepts. Many of these concepts, like role, elite, influence, system, subsystem and decision, were borrowed from other social sciences, or even the natural sciences. Much of the succeeding discussion in this book will be an attempt to define and relate these concepts. The concepts of current empirical theories, and their interrelations, comprise the responses to the questions that contemporary theorists pose. Fourth, the behavioralists advocated work on generalizations that would explain relationships among political phenomena. They wanted to further the development of a science of politics. Sorauf maintains that the behavioralists "have brought the hypothesis and theoretical proposition back into even narrowly circumscribed research."[3] He ends his discussion of the features of the behavioral movement by stating that the behavioralists wanted to infuse political science with new theoretical goals: ". . . they continue the search for the towering, over-all theoretical edifice which will integrate and unify the more specific findings and propositions of the discipline."[4] The purpose of this book is to discuss the most important efforts of current empirical political theorists to develop a "towering, over-all theoretical edifice." We are concerned with exploring the most general and ambitious statements about political affairs that behavioralists have developed.

In our investigation of the unifying and integrating theories of contemporary political science we will emphasize some relevant considerations and deemphasize others. The aspects of current political theories selected for special emphasis are the key questions posed by theorists, the concepts that they develop to respond to these questions, and the imaginative visions of the

---

[1] Frank J. Sorauf, *Perspectives on Political Science* (Columbus: Charles E. Merrill Publishing Co., 1965), p. 15.
[2] Sorauf, *Perspectives*, p. 15.
[3] Sorauf, *Perspectives*, pp. 15-16.
[4] Sorauf, *Perspectives*, p. 16.

political world implied in their sets of concepts. It has long been a favorite game and pastime of political scientists to criticize empirical theories for not measuring up to the model of an ideal and nonexistent political theory. The properties of an ideal political theory have been listed by the political theorist William H. Riker in his *Theory of Political Coalitions.*[5] Riker points out that the "intellectual edifice" of physical science is a "steady source of both inspiration and envy to scholars interested in the behavior of people rather than the motion of things."[6] Several features of the physical sciences account for their status as sources of inspiration and envy. First, the physical sciences "consist of a body of related and verified generalizations which describe occurrences accurately enough to be used for prediction."[7] Second, the generalizations are related because they are logically derived from a small set of axioms that constitute a consistent model of motion. According to most behavioralists, the ideal political theory would consist of a small set of axioms about political behavior, from which verifiable generalizations about political phenomena could be logically derived. At best, the generalizations would not only be verifiable, but they would be verified and reliable predictors. Needless to say, no current empirical theory of political activity comes close to fulfilling the standard set by the ideal political theory. Most current political theories, at least the "towering, over-all" varieties, are sets of concepts that provide a perspective on public affairs. They focus attention on some variables and problems and withdraw it from others. They provide categories under which wide varieties of particular political events can be subsumed. Finally, they provide abstract responses to highly general questions.

All of these features of current political theories place them in opposition to the ideal political theory. This has led some political scientists to claim that current political theories are not theories at all, but approaches, conceptual frameworks, paradigms, taxonomies, typologies or classification systems. This long standing debate about whether current empirical theories are really theories has proved to be one of the most arid academic exercises. We will call them theories in this book because they represent the most general statements of political relationships available in the contemporary world. However, it is important to keep in mind that we do not use the word theory to refer to the model of an ideal political theory. Thus, in our discussion of current political theories we will deemphasize the question of whether or not they contain consistent sets of axioms from which verifiable generalizations can be logically derived. Further, we will deemphasize the discussion of what kind of research projects would be necessary to make an adequate "test" of

[5] William H. Riker, *The Theory of Political Coalitions* (New Haven: Yale University Press, 1962).

[6] Riker, *The Theory of Political Coalitions*, p. 3.

[7] Riker, *The Theory of Political Coalitions*, p. 3.

the theory. Finally, we will deemphasize the problem of whether or not truly scientific theories are possible in political science. We are not concerned with mapping out strategies for extending old approaches or creating new ones. We are interested in the questions that political theorists have asked about political affairs and the responses that they have given to these questions. More than a generation has passed since World War II and an impressive body of empirical theory has been created. Perhaps it is time to investigate the content of this body of theory rather than its form.

Imaginative Perspectives

Every set of concepts that provides a category system for classifying political events contains an imaginative perspective on the political world. The student of behavioral political theories often loses sight of the fact that these theories represent attempts to generalize about politics. Often the theorist uses a specialized language that seems far removed from everyday political events and discourse. Frequently a technical vocabulary is necessary to isolate fine gradations of experience that ordinary language passes over. Mastery of the various technical vocabularies and the underlying category systems is not difficult once the student realizes that the concepts are being organized in response to a readily understandable question. Once the question and the concepts have been grasped, a more complete understanding of the theory can be gained by attempting to view the everyday political world from the perspective of the new concept system. One might ask, How would adopting this concept system as my working definition of politics alter my political perceptions and my political behavior? When approached from this viewpoint, each current political theory becomes a new way of orienting oneself to public affairs. A humanistic study of current political theories reveals that they contain insights as well as jargon.

Four types of political theories are discussed in this volume. Theories of political systems and poltical subsystems are concerned with how human organizations persist under stress. Theories of political influence are concerned with who is powerful and how groups and individuals attain power. Theories of contemporary democracy are concerned with the social and cultural conditions that sustain democratic regimes. All of these theories provide imaginative perspectives on political life and all of them can open up new possibilities for orienting oneself to public affairs.

Theories of the Political System

2

One of the interests that draws people into the study of politics is the desire to comprehend political life as a whole. In complex industrialized societies like the United States, politics appears in everyday life as a continuous process of conflict between individuals, groups, organizations and governments. Confronted by a mass of activity that seems to have little order, some political theorists attempt to get behind the appearances in an effort to discover principles that would make sense of the various conflicts. One of the ways of getting behind the surface conflicts of everyday political life is to search for the ways in which the conflicts are limited, or contained. Contemporary theories of the political system rest on the fundamental insight that every conflict is bounded by some agreement, whether tacit or explicit, and that every conflict has a discernible structure. For theorists of the political system, there is a way of understanding politics as a whole and interpreting the multitude of conflicts. The concept of political system is used to organize the confusing data of everyday political life, and has been thought out in response to a set of guiding questions that have interested American political theorists since the end of World War II. An understanding of these guiding questions will aid further comprehension of the various theories of the political system.

The Political Questions

Theorists of the political system have been primarily concerned with understanding how order is possible in human societies. The problem of order has been a traditional concern of political theorists in both the East and West. In the modern world it was Thomas Hobbes who first clearly formulated the problem of order. In his *Leviathan,* Hobbes argued that human beings have

been made so equal by nature that though "there be found one man sometimes manifestly stronger in body or of quicker mind than another, yet, when
all is reckoned together, the difference between man and man is not so
considerable as that one man can thereupon claim to himself any benefit to
which another may not pretend as well as he."[1] By equality Hobbes did not
mean a moral condition. Instead, he meant the factual condition that even
the weakest human being can kill the strongest, either through guile or alli-
ance with others, and the widespread knowledge among people of how to
take care of their own interests. Hobbes contended that in the absence of
effective government, this equality of ability led to an equality of hope
among people in the attaining of their ends. Thus, if "any two men desire the
same thing, which nevertheless they cannot both enjoy, they become
enemies; and in the way to their end, which is principally their own conserva-
tion, and sometimes their delectation only, endeavor to destroy or subdue
one another."[2] This is the foundation of the famous idea of a war where
"every man is enemy to every man," and the description of a human condition that is "solitary, poor, nasty, brutish, and short." For Hobbes, conflict
between human beings over scarce economic resources, esteem and power was
inevitable in the absence of a power that could overawe men through its
command of the means to coercion. Where no common power exists there is
continual "fear and danger of violent death." Hobbes argued that the fear of
punishment by an effective government was the only motive strong enough to
keep order among human beings.

Among contemporary political theorists the problem of order has received
serious attention. Theorists of the political system have asked these questions: How do political systems persist in a world of change? What is the level
of change with which a political system can effectively cope? How is the
range of choices restricted in human societies? Behind each of these questions
is a preoccupation with the problem of order. David Easton, who has devoted
his efforts to attempting to discover how political systems persist in a world of
change, argues that politics can best be viewed as a process through which
binding decisions on the distribution of scarce values are made for a society.
He envisions a human world in which people make demands upon society for
certain valued objects and actions. In Easton's view almost anything that
human beings want might be the object of a demand upon society under
some conditions. For Easton, the problem of order is defined in terms of the
problem of limiting the demands made upon society with respect to their
volume, their content and the way in which they are presented. If everyone

---

[1]Thomas Hobbes, *Leviathan: Parts I and II* (Indianapolis: The Bobbs-Merrill Company,
Inc., 1958), pp. 104-5.
[2]Hobbes, *Leviathan*, p. 105.

expected society at large to satisfy every wish, Easton implies, a Hobbesian situation in which every man was enemy to every man would result. In Easton's view, political systems fulfill the function of processing the demands that are made upon societies. Decisions of governments satisfy some demands and leave others frustrated. The problem of order is not resolved in the Hobbesian manner of postulating a government that strikes fear into the hearts of men. Instead, Easton argues that cultural norms restrict the content of demands that are pressed and social structures regulate the volume of demands that are processed. For Easton, political life is founded less on fear than on socialization into culturally approved patterns of behavior.

Karl Deutsch, who has sought to discover how political systems cope with change, visualizes governance as a process of guiding and steering human efforts towards the realization of social goals. Underlying the idea of steering is the notion that societies are subject to stress and require coordinated efforts to persist. For Deutsch, mechanisms for processing and interpreting information about dangers in the environment make an orderly society possible. David Apter, who argues that the problem of choice unites the sciences that study human beings and their relations with one another, defines politics as the processes through which choices are limited and contained in human societies. Like Easton, Apter implies that unrestricted choice would tear society apart. Explicitly, Apter follows Hobbes in arguing that human beings seek to rise as high as they can in the hierarchies of wealth, esteem and power. He states that people frequently press demands upon government to improve their positions in these hierarchies. If demands and possible alternatives were unrestricted, a war of all against all would ensue. As in Easton, order is not maintained through fear of the sovereign. Rather, cultural norms and values restrict the choices that occur to people and the ways that are legitimate to attain values, and social structures restrict the opportunities for pressing demands. Contemporary theorists of the political system have been investigating similar problems.

Is the problem of order the fundamental political question? One might object to current theories of the political system on the ground that they emphasize the problems of maintaining social stability over the problems of realizing desired social changes. None of the theorists of the political system has asked the question: How can political systems be changed? Certainly, there are at least two points of view through which the statics and dynamics of political systems can be analyzed. One may ask how political systems persist, or one may question how political systems change. However, the criticism that the problem of order emphasizes questions of political stability does not seem to be well taken. Implicit in a description of the factors that favor the persistence of political systems is an analysis of the tendencies that make for political change. While it is obvious that a concern with the problem of order does not make one a conservative, it is also true that discussions of the problem of order do not inadvertently bias political science in favor of stability and the current regime. To understand how order is maintained is also to comprehend how it can be disrupted.

Other objections to making the problem of order the fundamental political question concern the charge that it commits one to a specific theory of human nature and the argument that it does not adequately define the scope of politics. Our development of the problem of order was based on the analysis given it by Thomas Hobbes. Hobbes believed that in an environment characterized by scarce resources men would come into conflict over the distribution of goods. The ground, or basis, of this conflict was in human motivation. For Hobbes, men were motivated by appetite or desire, and aversion. Some appetites and aversions were inherited, as the appetite for food, and others proceeded "from experience and trial of their effects upon themselves or other men."[3] Essentially, Hobbes viewed men as self-seeking. Only fear of a greater power would prevent them from abusing their power. Contemporary theorists of the political system do not share the Hobbesian theory of motivation. They tend to be more behavioristic and hold that the process of socialization is the primary determinant of individual behavior. However, they veer toward a Hobbesian view of human nature when they argue that unless alternatives of choice or the permissible content and volume of demands are culturally restricted, order will collapse. As a counter to the systems theorists one might argue that cultural values and norms that limit alternatives of choice and the ways in which choice can be exercised are often biased in favor of the groups that are most powerful in a given society. One might contend that if exploitation was eliminated the "human nature" that was visible in an exploitative society would be replaced by a human nature characterized by creativity and love. There is no conclusive evidence to justify embracing with certainty any view of human nature, or the view that human beings do not have a nature. At least the field is open enough that it is not necessary to accept the Hobbesian view that seems to be implied in the writings of contemporary theorists of the political system.

The final serious objection to making the problem of order the fundamental political question concerns the argument that it does not adequately define the scope of politics. When we considered the charge that the problem of order committed one to a specific view of human nature, we noted that an opponent of systems theories might argue that the content of cultural values and norms can be interpreted as an expression of the interests of the most powerful groups in a society. This remark opens the way for considering whether or not the problem of order adequately accounts for the phenome-

---

[3] Hobbes, *Leviathan*, p. 53.

non of power. If we take the problem of order in its most general sense—How is order possible in human societies?—then there is no reason why it should not account for power. Effectively organized control over property, the means to coercion and the means of communication comprise important bases for ordering human societies. It is less the problem of order itself than the limited solutions to it that fail to cover the entire scope of politics. The Hobbesian idea that the fear of force is the primary determinant of order and the notion of systems theorists that the effective socialization of people into cultural patterns is the primary determinant of order are both too restrictive. Fear and enculturation are both important factors in the maintenance of order, but so are organized control of the means to power and, perhaps, freely given loyalty. Presumably, the relative effect of each one of these factors for the preservation of order will vary by society. Thus, the objections that the problem of order contains a built-in bias toward conservatism and that it fails to cover the entire scope of politics are ill-founded. The claim that the problem of order commits one to a specific view of human nature seems to be much more warranted, although theorists of the political system are not clear about their interpretation of the human being.

The Political System

While theorists of the political system have concerned themselves mainly with the problem of order, they have not all defined the political system in the same way. Since each systems theorist employs a different theoretical vocabulary and a slightly different set of concepts, it is wisest to consider each interpretation of the political system separately and make generalizations about systems theory as we go along. However, even though it would not be worthwhile to discuss systems theory in general before we have reviewed particular analyses of political life, we may say a few words about some basic distinctions to keep in mind as the discussion proceeds.

Most theorists of the political system follow the biologist von Bertalanffy in defining a system generally as a "set of units with relationships among them."[4] This definition is general enough to cover work that is done in such diverse fields as mechanical engineering, biology and the social sciences. What the units are that make up the system and what relationships among them exist are matters for theorists and researchers in the particular fields to settle. It should be clear that one can call any set of units a system and proceed to explore the relationships among them. Thus, in some systems a multitude of interesting relationships will obtain and in others a few uninteresting relationships will be present. The object, of course, is to define meaningfully related

---

[4]W. J. M. Mackenzie, *Politics and Social Science* (Baltimore: Penguin Books, 1967), p. 100.

units. The adoption of the concept "system" does not solve any significant theoretical problems. It merely provides a term under which discussion about political life as a whole can take place.

In the discussion of systems in political theory, two sets of distinctions seem to be important. First, there is the distinction between membership systems and analytic systems. The units of membership systems are whole human beings or societies, while the units of analytic systems are types of action. Most theorists of the political system discuss analytic systems. Second, there is the distinction between systems that have processes for changing the relationships among their units and systems that do not have this capacity. Easton and Deutsch discuss creative systems, while Kaplan discusses systems whose rules remain the same. While these two sets of distinctions should be kept in mind, they are not as important as the concepts referring to the "political" aspect of political systems. It is with political life that our discussion is primarily concerned.

David Easton

For many political scientists empirical theories of the political system as a whole are identified with the work of David Easton. In his *The Political System,* published in 1953, Easton argued that political scientists should develop theories of political behavior that would explain events that occur in public life.[5] He suggested that political theorists should place more emphasis on elaborating explanations of behavior and less emphasis on describing the history of political ideas and passing moral judgments on politics. Thus, Easton became one of the most important figures in the behavioral movement, which sought to make the study of politics a more scientific discipline. Since 1953 Easton has developed an ambitious theory of political life that incorporates a guiding question about public affairs, an interrelated set of concepts about politics and an imaginative perspective on the political world. In 1965 Easton's two major works up to the present, *A Framework for Political Analysis* and *A Systems Analysis of Political Life,* were published.[6] In *A Framework for Political Analysis* Easton discussed in detail the kind of theory that would fulfill the requirements that he had set in *The Political System.* Our discussion will be concerned primarily with *A Systems Analysis of Political Life,* which contains Easton's theory of the political system.

---

[5] David Easton, *The Political System* (New York: Alfred A. Knopf, Inc., 1953).
[6] David Easton, *A Framework for Political Analysis* (Englewood Cliffs: Prentice-Hall, Inc., 1965). David Easton, *A Systems Analysis of Political Life* (New York: John Wiley and Sons, Inc., 1965).

The Political Question

Easton has been deeply concerned with the problem of formulating a guiding question around which empirical research and theory construction could be organized. He has recognized that all scientific inquiry starts with a question, and that the substance of the question that the scientist asks will significantly determine the phenomena that he observes and the relations that he discovers. For example, political scientists would observe primarily documents and discover relations between formal structures of government if they were guided in their work by the question, What are the differences and similarities among written constitutions? They would not observe the processes of conflict that occur in the struggle to determine legislation, nor would they observe the attitudes that individuals have about politics. They would not study the relationships of power or the formal institutions in preliterate societies, nor would they investigate the dynamics of international relations. Perhaps most important, they would never learn whether or not the rules specified in constitutions were followed in practice. This does not mean that one should not study the differences and similarities among written constitutions. It does mean that there are many interesting political problems that such a study would exclude, and that one might think of a question that would lead to the investigation of constitutions as well as inquiry into other problems. A good question to guide research and theory construction would allow students of politics to observe a wide range of interesting phenomena and find significant relations among them.

David Easton believes that he has formulated a question that meets the requirements of wide scope and orientation toward significant relations. He has sought to express a question that would encourage communication between students of the politics of preliterate societies, organizations, communities, nation states and international systems. With this comprehensive aim in mind he has suggested that political scientists and empirical political theorists be guided by the question, "How does it come about that any type of system can persist at all, even under the pressures of frequent or constant crisis?"[7] He has contrasted this question with another query that many political scientists have considered fundamental, "Who gets what, when, and how?"[8] Easton contends that the problem of determining who benefits from political activity takes for granted the existence of a political system which provides the context in which conflict over economic rewards, control of human actions and resources, and esteem takes place.[9] Conflict among

---

[7]Easton, *A Systems Analysis*, p. vii.
[8]Harold Lasswell, *Politics: Who Gets What, When, How* (Cleveland: The World Publishing Company, 1958).
[9]Easton, *A Systems Analysis*, p. 475.

human beings is not random; it is always patterned and limited by norms. The question of how any type of system can persist at all directs one to study the overall context as well as the apparent struggles. Thus, the question of persistence through change orients the student of politics to observe more phenomena than does the question of who benefits, and it relates the struggle for benefits to the rules and processes that regulate it. Easton's question also permits the investigation and comparison of all types of political systems, whether or not we morally approve of them. Democracies and dictatorships are both subject to stress. Both also often persist through time and change. While there are differences between the structural problems that democracies and dictatorships encounter in coping with stress, they are political regimes that presuppose a political system.

Before we can discuss how it is possible for political systems to persist, éven under the pressures of frequent or constant crisis, we must understand what Easton means by the term political system. Easton has defined a political system as those interactions "through which values are authoritatively allocated for a society."[10] Since Easton considers a system as "any set of variables regardless of the degree of interrelationship among them," the variables relevant to our discussion here are interactions, or relationships, between human beings.[11] It is important to note that the relevant variables in the study of politics are called interactions. This means that, for Easton, political scientists study cross sections of the activity of many human beings rather than whole personalities. The activities in which the political scientist is interested cluster around the processes through which values are authoritatively allocated for a society. The authoritative allocation of values means the binding commitment of resources and actions toward the attainment of goals for an entire society. Thus, concrete human beings move in and out of the political system depending on whether or not they are participating in the defining process. We stress the fact that Easton is studying interactions rather than concrete human beings because it is the basis of thinking of politics from the point of view of the system rather than from the point of view of the individual. Easton will interpret events in political life in terms of their consequences for the authoritative allocation of values for a society and not in terms of their direct effects on human beings. It is often difficult for people to think of themselves as sets of cross sections of activity. In the common sense world we view ourselves as thinking, feeling and acting beings integrated by a consciousness and living among others. We normally do not interpret our actions in terms of their bearing on the persistence of a process for making binding commitments of resources and actions for a society. Yet we must make just such an interpretation if we wish to understand what Easton means by a political system.

---

[10] Easton, *A Systems Analysis*, p. 21.
[11] Easton, *A Systems Analysis*, p. 21.

There are several problems with Easton's definition of the political system, most of which concern the concept of authority. For Easton authority is a type of power relationship "based on the expectation that if A sends a message to B—which may be called a wish, suggestion, regulation, law, command, order, or the like—B will adopt it as the premise of his own behavior."[12] Thus, the discussion of authority does not concern the reasons people obey. It is concerned solely with the flow of activity involved in the processes of command and obedience, and does not concentrate on those relationships in which the subordinate believes that obedience is morally justified, or legitimate. In itself there is nothing wrong with this definition of authority. Definitions cannot be judged right or wrong except in the contexts of their utility for furthering inquiry and their consistency with other concepts in a given theory. In Easton's case, his definition of authority is not consistent with his other concepts. Easton would like to distinguish between authority and power. He states that in every political system there are "vital non-authority roles" through which wants are converted to binding allocations. He contends that the relative influence of authority and nonauthority roles in political activity "will depend upon the particular circumstances."[13] Yet Easton has defined a political system as those interactions through which values are authoritatively allocated for a society. If authority is the probability that B will adopt A's command as the premise of his own behavior, it is not possible to speak consistently about vital nonauthority roles through which wants are converted to binding allocations. Easton would like to maintain a distinction between "the authorities" and the men of power. This is a distinction that we often make in everyday talk about politics. However, his definition of the political system is too ambiguous to allow him to maintain that distinction. Ambiguities in political theories, as in all scientific and philosophical work, are dangerous because they allow an author to change the meaning of a term at his convenience. Either the authoritative allocation of values is performed by actors who are culturally expected to perform this function, or the authoritative allocation of values is performed by anyone whose commands about a public activity are obeyed. If one takes the first position, he has the advantage of being able to analyze relatively stable roles in the political system and the disadvantage of possibly ignoring some binding allocations. If one takes the second position, he has the advantage of being able to describe binding allocations and the disadvantage of dissolving roles into power relationships. One cannot consistently straddle the fence and attempt to take both positions at once.

The difficulty in Easton's definition of the political system is related to the guiding political question that he asks. He criticizes the question of who gets what, when, and how because it assumes a context in which conflict over

---

[12] Easton, *A Systems Analysis*, p. 207.
[13] Easton, *A Systems Analysis*, p. 210.

benefits takes place. That context is the set of roles that defines the process of authoritatively allocating values for a society. However, cultural expectations about who makes decisions about committing resources and actions to the attainment of societal goals do not always define who actually does make binding decisions and how they are made. Does this mean that Easton's theory is useless to study for those who seek to explain events in political life, and that Easton's question will not orient an investigator toward significant relationships among phenomena? Such conclusions would be mistaken. The most that we can say now is that when we study other parts of Easton's theory we must be alert to the definition of authority that is implied, and that we need not accept Easton's contention that his question is the most inclusive one that can be posed.

The Fundamental Concepts

Any ambitious political theory is much more than a statement of a question and a definition of the range of the phenomena that will be considered. It is also a set of general categories in which data can be classified and a statement of relationships between these categories. At best, the relationships that the theorist describes will provide a satisfactory answer to the questions that he has raised.

For Easton, the fundamental concepts of his political theory are system, input, demand, support, output and feedback. We have already seen that Easton defines a political system as those interactions through which values are authoritatively allocated for a society, and we have pointed out a problem with this definition. In addition to this definition Easton has several important remarks to make about the political system in its most general aspect. First, since he is concerned with discovering how it comes about that political systems persist, even under the pressures of frequent or constant crisis, he proposes to investigate "the life processes of political systems—those fundamental functions without which no system could endure—together with the typical modes of response through which systems manage to sustain them."[14] Thus, political systems perform certain functions and are exposed to stress in their operation. Stress is of particular significance because political systems are open; they are exposed to influences from other social systems. Political systems do not merely adapt to influences from their environments. They respond to disturbances sometimes by altering their internal structure and sometimes by acting to alter the environments in which they are embedded. Easton's essential view of political systems is not mechanistic. He contends that "a political system shares with all other social systems [an] extraordinarily variable capacity to respond to the conditions under which it

---

[14] Easton, *A Systems Analysis*, p. 17.

functions."[15] However, it is vital to understand that Easton does not view the political system as an organism and, particularly, not as an organism with a mind. The political system is a pattern of interactions that may make sense to an observer. When political systems respond to stresses they respond through human beings and not as separate units. It is a cross section of a multitude of activities that makes sense, not an independent social or group mind. Also, it is important to keep in mind that political systems need not always be successful in coping with stress.

Although Easton is investigating the functions performed by political systems, he does not claim that every aspect of a given political system tends to further the system's persistence. One consequence of the plasticity of political systems, or their capacity to respond to the conditions under which they function, is the possibility that their internal structures may be in conflict. Further, stresses from the environment may cause the interactions that make up the system to dissolve. In this case an organic analogy is not out of place. Just as the biological system of the human being cannot adapt to a bullet in the heart, a political system would be unlikely to adapt to the loss of all of the male members of the society for which it allocates values. In short, political systems have limits of tolerance to stress and internal conflict.

Political systems have two functions: they allocate values for a society and they induce most members to accept these allocations as binding, at least most of the time.[16] The political system can be visualized as a process that converts demands of the members of a society into binding allocations. Even more generally, we can think of the political system as a process that converts inputs into outputs and feeds the outputs back into the environment. While this language from general systems theory may not be familiar in ordinary political discourse, all of Easton's concepts refer to political phenomena and occurrences that we can readily identify. Terms like input, demand, support, output and feedback abstract from raw political activity certain general characteristics and provide the means of relating these characteristics to one another. Once we understand what characteristics Easton includes in these concepts we will be able to appreciate the special angle of vision through which Easton looks at public life. Easton's political vocabulary does not merely constitute a set of technical terms that reproduce exactly the characteristics named by terms in everyday political language. Rather, it orders political activity in a new way.

The most convenient starting point for a discussion of the political process is an analysis of the concept *input*. For Easton, input is a term that refers to everything in the environment of a political system that is relevant to political stress.[17] Thus, input is a concept that is especially relevant to Easton's politi-

---

[15] Easton, *A Systems Analysis*, p. 18.
[16] Easton, *A Systems Analysis*, pp. 23-24.
[17] Easton, *A Systems Analysis*, p. 26.

cal theory. Since he is primarily interested in discovering how political systems persist in changing environments, Easton develops concepts that are specifically related to furthering his particular inquiry. Inputs summarize all of the activities and events that either contribute to the persistence of modes of allocating values for a society, or threaten the persistence of such processes. Inputs may be further classified as *demands* and *supports*. A *demand* may be defined as an "expression of opinion that an authoritative allocation with regard to a particular subject matter should or should not be made by those responsible for doing so."[18] Demands are the components of the political process that provide the process with its justification. If individuals and groups did not seek to have the society fulfill some of their desires there would be no need for a system that authoritatively allocated values for that society. Further, unless conflict over demands occurred between individuals and groups, there would be no need for binding allocations because everyone would agree about what should be done. Thus, Easton remarks that if we could find a system in which no demands were made, we could be "certain that the system was in the process of disintegrating."[19]

However, while there would be no political system without the expression of demands, demands also constitute a source of stress for the system. Just because demands represent unfulfilled wants, the political system will be taxed in any efforts to process them. This paradox underlies Easton's entire analysis. The very elements that make the political system necessary are also the elements that threaten its persistence. Demands may constitute a source of stress on the political system in several ways. If demands cannot be fulfilled support for the system will decline. Sometimes demands are not met because there are too many of them for the system to process. At other times demands are not met because they are incompatible with other demands that are being processed. If a political system is not to collapse from the weight of too many demands or the stresses created by incompatible demands, cultural norms must be developed that place limits on the content of the demands that are made, the people in the society who can express demands and the ways in which demands are expressed. Thus, the first reason political systems persist through change is that cultural norms limit stress by controlling the flow of demands.

The second type of input that Easton discusses is support. *Support* is present when someone orients himself favorably toward another or when someone acts on behalf of another. The other may be a person, group, goal, idea or institution.[20] Support is directed to what Easton calls "the basic

---

[18] Easton, *A Systems Analysis*, p. 38.
[19] Easton, *A Systems Analysis*, p. 48.
[20] Easton, *A Systems Analysis*, p. 159.

EASTON'S MODEL OF THE POLITICAL SYSTEM

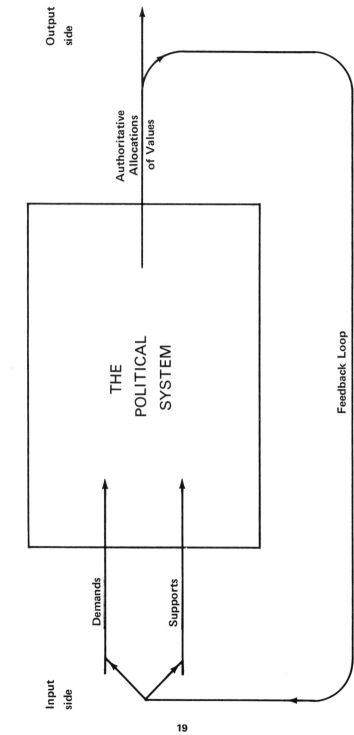

Input
side

Output
side

Demands

Supports

THE
POLITICAL
SYSTEM

Authoritative
Allocations
of Values

Feedback Loop

political objects." These basic political objects can be classified as the political community, the regime and the authorities. Easton defines the political community as that "aspect of a political system that consists of its members seen as a group of persons bound together by a political division of labor."[21] In other words, a political community is a group of persons for whom authoritative allocations of value are made. People support a political community when they believe or act on the principle that a given group should have a political system of its own. Support for the political community is usually the most generalized support present in a political system.

The regime is a set of values that a political system should actualize, a set of norms defining permitted and prohibited actions in the political system, and an authority structure. Thus, the meaning of regime approximates the everyday meaning of "form of government." Regime values are culturally defined expectations of the goals that a political system will seek. Easton is not saying that political systems *ought* to meet certain demands rather than others, or undertake any specific projects. Rather, he is claiming that every culture defines goals that the political system is supposed to attain. Similarly, regime norms do not define a set of absolute moral rights and wrongs. They too are the cultural expectations of proper behavior in a given political system. People support a regime when they believe in the rightness of the relevant values, norms or authority structure, or when they act to attain these values, fulfill these norms or respect this authority structure. The authorities are the occupants of roles clustered around the process of authoritatively allocating values for a society. They are the people who are expected to process demands in accordance with the values and norms of the regime. People support the authorities through approval or acceptance of what they do.

Support may be diffuse or specific. Specific support is given in return for the fulfillment of demands. Easton argues that if all support were specific the great majority of political systems could not persist. Political systems arise because all demands cannot be met, and because contradictory demands appear in social living. Thus, in "every system, part of the readiness to tolerate outputs that are perceived to run contrary to one's wants and demands, flows from a general or diffuse attachment to regime and community."[22] Diffuse support for the authorities and the regime can be expressed as a belief in the rightness or legitimacy of personnel and rules, belief that there is a common interest that overrides individual wants, and a sense of community with other members of the political system. Support may be directed toward one or more of the basic political objects and withdrawn from the others. Negative support, or opposition, can also be directed toward one or more of

---

[21] Easton, *A Systems Analysis*, p. 177.
[22] Easton, *A Systems Analysis*, p. 272.

the basic political objects. Support is a concept developed to aid in answering the question: Why do political systems persist, even under the pressures of frequent or constant crisis? When we discussed demands we noted that cultural norms limit stress on the political system by controlling the flow of demands. Our analysis of support has made this point much more intelligible. Diffuse support for the cultural norms, as well as for regime values and the authorities, makes it possible for the norms to limit stress. Thus, the second reason why political systems persist through change is that diffuse support for the political community, the regime and the authorities checks people from opposing the political system each time their specific demands are not met.

The study of inputs constitutes only half of the analysis of the political process. Demands directed at the authorities, or formulated by some of the authorities, are processed and fed back into the environment as outputs. *Outputs* are authoritative allocations of values, or decisions of the authorities about the goals to which the human and material resources of a society will be committed. In general they are responses to demands and represent efforts to meet or suppress them. Implicit in the notion of output is the third reason political systems persist through change. When the specific demands of people and groups in the society have been met or effectively suppressed, or when people and groups believe that their demands have been met or that they are unattainable, specific support for, or acquiescence in, the political system is generated. Political systems persist through change because they can meet demands, or appear to meet them, and thereby generate specific support.

Once he has specified the reasons political systems persist through change, Easton continues to develop his analysis one more step. In order to perform their function of authoritatively allocating values, the authorities must gain information about the state of support within the society and the consequences of their outputs. The general function of *feedback* is to supply this information. For Easton, feedback is an essential concept to the understanding of political systems. He believes that the "dominant and most fertile intellectual innovation of our own age has been that of information feedback."[23] It is equivalent in importance to Newton's laws of motion and Darwin's theory of evolution, both of which had profound effects as analogies in the study of man and society. In a political context, feedback provides the means through which the political system is enabled to cope with stress. Insofar as the results of outputs are communicated back to the authorities without distortion, they have the opportunity to respond to stress by varying authoritative allocations or even changing the values, norms and authority structure of the regime. In an extreme situation, response may involve altering the political community itself, as in the case of secession. Easton is

---

[23] Easton, *A Systems Analysis*, p. 367.

unclear about when a response becomes so drastic that one can say that the political system has dissolved and another one has taken its place. He is certain that authorities can make creative responses to stressful situations, and that adequate feedback is an important factor in determining whether successful creative responses are possible. Underlying the cultural norms that control the flow of demands, the diffuse support for the basic political objects and the actual or perceived fulfillment of specific demands is the flow of communication from members of the society to authorities and from authorities to the members of the society. Communication here is a very general concept that means much more than the use of spoken and written language. Authorities can communicate to people through arresting them and people can communicate to authorities through rioting. There is some information relayed in any action that forms a part of a human relationship. With the concepts of feedback and communication Easton attains the most general level of political analysis.

Imaginative Perspective

Edmund Dahlstrom has remarked that it is interesting how the idea of society as a cybernetic (information or communications) system has been stressed in "centrally controlled societies such as the USSR."[24] This does not mean that Easton's theory can be used as a convenient support for totalitarian political practice. Rather, it is a comment on how contemporary life in the industrialized world, which is set in large-scale and impersonal organizations, may influence the way that we interpret political events. While Easton's purpose was to develop a set of categories that would allow him to answer the question, "How does it come about that any type of system can persist at all, even under the pressures of frequent or constant crisis?", in the process of defining these categories he articulated an imaginative perspective on political life that we can enter once we have understood his concepts and their relations to one another. What is this perspective, and what does it tell us about the choices that we can make in our political existence?

  The first step toward imaginatively understanding Easton's political world is to take the point of view of the political system. One might conceive of himself as a set of cross sections of activity, some of which have bearing on the persistence of the political system and others of which are performed outside of the process through which values are authoritatively allocated for the society. One must view those of his activities that are politically relevant as demands that might threaten the existence of the political system and as supports that might contribute to the system's persistence. He must judge the policies and decisions of the authorities not by their effects on his purposes,

---

[24] Edmund Dahlstrom, "Sociology and Society," *Acta Sociologica* 12 (1969): 89.

but by their consequences as stress-producing or stress-reducing outputs. Finally, one must think of his responses to politics as feedback to the authorities who will use the information to make creative adjustments in the system. In all, taking the point of view of the system is both unfamiliar and unsatisfying. Is there any benefit in imaginatively participating in Easton's perspective?

Taking the point of view of the system diminishes the significance of the individual human being as a unit of political analysis, but it may help liberate him as a political actor. When one understands how demands threaten the political system and how supports help maintain it, he may begin to question his attitudes toward and his actions in political life. One may ask why he obeys the cultural norms that limit the content and flow of demands, why he extends diffuse support to the political community, the regime and the authorities and why he is satisfied with some outputs rather than others. The person who asks these questions need not decide that the norms are bankrupt, that the support for the basic political objects has been betrayed and that he has received an unjust allocation of values. He may decide to extend even greater and more intelligent support to the different levels of the political system. However, whether he decides to increase, diminish or maintain his support for the basic political objects, he will understand that his attitudes and actions have significance from another point of view than his personal one. This is the major contribution of Easton's systems analysis to interpreting everyday political life. Regime values and norms function not only to satisfy or deprive human beings. They also function to maintain the political system, or the process through which values are authoritatively allocated for a society. The intelligent political man must judge for himself whether or not the rules through which values are allocated are just. Taking the point of view of the political system does not mean worshipping the political system. On the contrary, it should mean the expansion of one's experience and the facilitation of his action.

Morton A. Kaplan

In the field of international relations, systems theories of politics have been advanced through the work of Morton A. Kaplan. In *System and Process in International Politics* Kaplan developed a view of political systems based on engineering concepts and presented several alternative models of international relations.[25] Since 1957, when *System and Process* was published, Kaplan has worked on a wide variety of projects. He has undertaken disciplined historical case study analysis, attempted computer simulations of some of his models,

---

[25] Morton A. Kaplan, *System and Process in International Politics* (New York: John Wiley and Sons, 1957).

engaged in the study of international law, created a nightmarish vision of a future technological society and speculated on a philosophical and ethical foundation for contemporary political science. More than most current empirical theorists, Kaplan is within the great tradition of political analysis that combines thought on problems of value with observation and categorization of social phenomena. Kaplan does not believe that the study of man and his relations can proceed on the principle that facts and values can be separated into two unbridgeable conceptual realms. He argues that values are grounded in empirically determinable needs. This position divides him from many other empirical theorists who promote the idea that statements of fact can be empirically verified while statements about values merely express preferences. In *Macropolitics* Kaplan has presented a restatement of part of the systems theory that he worked out in *System and Process,* as well as an account of many of the other projects with which he has been occupied.[26] Thus, the focus of our attention will be on the arguments that are developed in *Macropolitics.*

The Political Question

Unlike David Easton, one question has not dominated the thought of Morton Kaplan. Perhaps this is because Kaplan does not interpret the problem of a theory of politics in the same way as Easton. Kaplan does not believe that there can be a general theory of political systems. He argues that there is "no such thing as theory in general; there is only theory about some specific subject matter."[27] Thus, Kaplan's work is directed toward solving problems that are more specifically defined than the determination of how political systems persist through change. For Kaplan the attempt to develop a theory of politics is doomed to failure not only because of empirical complexity but because of the logic of scientific investigation. One can investigate and generalize about the dynamics of balance of power politics or the tensions present in a world dominated by two competing nuclear powers, but one can never scientifically investigate an abstraction such as politics in general. While Kaplan's point appears to be persuasive, we should realize that terms such as "balance of power politics" are abstractions in the same way as "politics." If the various specific systems that Kaplan analyzes have certain processes in common, these processes could be the basis of a general theory of political activity.

Kaplan also differs from Easton in his interpretation of the relation between the concepts of systems theory and political phenomena. Kaplan defines a system simply as a "set of variables related by one or more func-

---

[26] Morton A. Kaplan, *Macropolitics* (Chicago: Aldine Publishing Company, 1969).
[27] Kaplan, *Macropolitics,* p. 71.

tions."[28] He adds that although "the world is open, the systems model is always closed."[29] By this comment Kaplan commits himself to a view that separates systems descriptions of political phenomena from the political phenomena themselves, in a way foreign to Easton. Easton argued that political systems are open, adaptive and creative. He thought that they could respond to stress by altering their structures as well as by changing their environments. While Kaplan does not doubt that political structures change and that political variables can affect other social variables, he contends that political theories cannot attempt to mirror the world and still be explanatory. From Kaplan's viewpoint, a theory of a particular political system will describe a configuration of actors and specify a set of essential rules of relation among these actors. Insofar as any actual political situation approaches the conditions specified by such a model, the model will be useful for describing and predicting the dynamics of that situation. When the actual political situation changes so that new rules of relation among actors apply, the model will no longer be a useful predictor. While Easton attempts to build political change into his theory, Kaplan believes that political theorists are not yet sophisticated enough to account for change from one set of essential rules to another. In rough translation, Kaplan would not try to account for changes in political community or regime. This is a consequence of his view that it is vain to try to develop a general theory of politics.

Kaplan's focus of interest is consistent with his relatively modest expectations for political theory. He states that the "major task facing social science" is to "locate and describe the stimuli which will evoke . . . various mechanisms in different systems."[30] Thus, Kaplan asks several guiding questions. First, he would like to describe the basic types of political systems. Second, he would like to define the fundamental political processes that occur in all systems. Third, he would like to relate process to structure by discovering which kinds of systems emphasize which processes. Although Kaplan's discussion of the nature of political theory denies the possibility of a general theory of political activity, the major task facing social science that he identifies implies such a theory at its successful conclusion.

The Fundamental Concepts

Kaplan's concepts are relevant to the task that he has set for the social sciences. At the most general level, Kaplan has developed a set of concepts that define the kinds of systems useful for describing political situations. Defining a system as a set of variables related by one or more functions,

---

[28] Kaplan, *Macropolitics*, p. 25.
[29] Kaplan, *Macropolitics*, p. 25.
[30] Kaplan, *Macropolitics*, p. 156.

Kaplan states that political systems are both ultrastable and multistable. An ultrastable system can "employ negative feedback both to reduce disturbances in the environment and to reorganize itself in a way that maintains some system variable within defined limits."[31] We are familiar with the notion of feedback from our discussion of Easton's theory. The term *negative feedback* refers to information that threatens the integrity of the system. An ultrastable system can process information about threats in such a way that it is enabled to respond to maintain its integrity within specified limits. A multistable system has "one or more part systems that are themselves ultrastable."[32] The term *actor* refers to a system that participates in a larger system. Multistable systems can be system dominant or subsystem dominant. In the case of system dominance explanations of the behavior of the system do not have to incorporate information relevant to the subsystems. For example, an explanation of the price of newspapers does not have to take into account information about the specific personalities of newspaper readers. In the case of subsystem dominance explanations of the behavior of the system must incorporate information relevant to the subsystems. The international systems that Kaplan has studied are relatively subsystem dominant in that the particular characteristics of the actors determine in large part the dynamics of the system. For example, in an international system composed of two blocs led by nuclear powers, the type of regime characteristic of each power would be important in determining the relations between them. The political system itself has a particular function in the social system within which it is embedded. The political system has "the metatask capacity to act as the ultrastable regulator of the larger system in which it functions."[33] While task capacity is the "ability to reduce environmental disturbances," metatask capacity is "the ability to reorganize either oneself or the external environment in such a way that the disturbances do not arise, at least in the same form as before."[34]

Kaplan's lexicon can be translated so that some connection is made with everyday political language. When he states that the political system has the metatask capacity to act as the ultrastable regulator of the larger system in which it functions, Kaplan is saying that the function of the political system is to organize activity aimed at preserving the integrity of the social system and to plan against threats to the integrity of the social system. The political system also functions to preserve its own integrity. This is its task capacity. Thus, when Easton investigated how political systems persist through change he was concerned with the task capacity of political systems. There is no

---

[31] Kaplan, *Macropolitics*, p. 25.
[32] Kaplan, *Macropolitics*, p. 25.
[33] Kaplan, *Macropolitics*, p. 67.
[34] Kaplan, *Macropolitics*, p. 73.

equivalence between the functions that Easton and Kaplan assign to the political system with reference to the social system. Easton defined politics as the authoritative allocation of values for a society, while Kaplan defines politics as the organization of activities aimed at maintaining the society from danger. While both definitions purport to identify the essential function of political activity, they seem to be based on partial perspectives. Within any society politics may appear to be the process through which decisions are made on the commitment of resources and activities to goals. However, in relations between societies politics may appear as the process through which societies attempt to preserve and extend their integrities. Kaplan's general thought on political systems shows influences from his preoccupation with international politics.

Once Kaplan has described the kinds of systems that are most useful for describing and predicting political affairs, he turns to the description of the fundamental processes that occur in such systems. Kaplan notes that a system can act "to satisfy needs only by employing a mechanism which scans for, transmits, and utilizes information."[35] Every mechanism involved with meta-task capacity has the function of satisfying the system's needs. However, a mechanism can become "pathological" when it produces "structural changes in the system which later filter out needed information and thereby prevent successful adaptation by the system to its environment."[36] In his discussion of regulatory mechanisms, Kaplan draws heavily upon concepts from Freudian theories of psychoanalysis. In general, Kaplan proposes that the same mechanisms that regulate personality systems regulate social and political systems. He bases his proposal on the observation that both personality and political systems are multistable. Kaplan isolates the mechanisms of catharsis, cathexis, learning, displacement, repression, frustration, sublimation, projection, introjection, identification, and apathy and isolation as standard regulatory processes. These terms, which are familiar in the literature of psychoanalysis, need some explanation when applied to political systems. All of the mechanisms define ways in which information can be processed. Since societies process information as well as individuals, the mechanisms should characterize both kinds of systems. An example will show how this is possible. Individuals often repress desires that they cannot satisfy. Such desires never come into consciousness and information relevant to them is screened out. When a desire arising from a persistent need is repressed, personality conflict will ensue. Political systems can also engage in repression. Through censorship and other denials of freedom of expression information about the content and desirability of certain policies can be repressed. A political system might repress information about certain policies because a

---

[35] Kaplan, *Macropolitics*, p. 140.
[36] Kaplan, *Macropolitics*, p. 140.

powerful neighbor would threaten the system if those policies were publicly expressed. It might also repress such information to preserve its own integrity.

Kaplan has made some suggestions about how the structures and processes might be correlated. Whether or not a political system was system dominant or subsystem dominant would be important to determining which processes came into play, as would information about whether or not the system was directed to maximize specified goals. For example, Kaplan has predicted that subsystem dominant nondirective systems will tend to use repression less than system dominant nondirective systems. Tendency statements such as this one seem to depend on a theory of the relationship between system type and frequency of process that Kaplan has not yet developed. Such a theory is implicit in Kaplan's critique of Easton. Kaplan argues that to say that political systems tend to persist is not to say that all systems will succeed in persisting. The important research problem is to discover which factors are involved in the capacity to persist and "how these factors vary with the kinds of systems and kinds of environments."[37]

Thus far, Kaplan's major applications of systems theory have been made in the field of international politics. In line with his three guiding questions, Kaplan has attempted to describe the basic types of political systems that appear in international relations, the fundamental political processes that occur in these systems and the relation of these processes to the structural characteristics of the respective systems. For the study of systems in international politics, Kaplan has suggested the use of five key sets of variables: the essential rules of the system, the transformation rules of the system, the actor classificatory variables, the capability variables, and the information variables. The essential rules of the system are defined by the patterns of activity necessary to the maintenance of equilibrium within the system. They are essential in the sense that if they are not fulfilled in action the system no longer exists. This is another way of saying that the essential rules of the system are themselves the definition of the system. Thus, maintaining equilibrium within the system means seeing that the essential rules of the system are fulfilled in action. The "transformation rules state the changes that occur in the system as inputs across the boundary of the system that differ from those required for equilibrium move the system either toward instability or toward the stability of a new system."[38] The concept of transformation rules is an attempt to approach the problem of system change, which Kaplan had earlier declared insoluble at the present stage of development in political theory. Transformation rules would state the general principles through which one set of essential rules changes to another set of essential rules.

---

[37] Kaplan, *Macropolitics*, p. 70.
[38] Kaplan, *Macropolitics*, pp. 212-13.

Kaplan remarks that while the concept of transformation rules is the least developed aspect of systems models of international politics, if perfected it would supply political theorists with models of dynamic change. The actor classificatory variables state the structural characteristics of the actors within the given system. Thus, in a small group, such as a family, the actors may be identified as concrete human beings, while in a national political system the actors may be identified as people performing roles that are relevant to the stipulated function of the system. With respect to international political systems, the actors may be identified as nation states, blocs of nation states, empires or other transpersonal collectivities. Kaplan makes the important point that whether the actors making up a system are human beings, occupants of roles or collectivities, they do not "behave consonantly with the essential rules merely to maintain equilibrium but because they are motivated under the specified system conditions to do so."[39] The linkage between motivation of the units and the maintenance of the system is one of the major problems of theories of political systems and also one of the questions that is least thoroughly explored. Besides stating that the actors must be motivated to maintain equilibrium in social systems, Kaplan does very little in the way of describing how such motivation is attained. The capability variables state the means and resources for action commanded by the actors within the system. For example, the acquisition of nuclear armaments by one or more parties to an international relation is likely to be of great importance in determining the pattern of that relation. While the actor classificatory variables define the unit of action within the system, the capability variables define the means employed by units of action as they follow the essential rules of the system or transform them. Finally, the information variables define the knowledge possessed by the actors about the state of the system. Information variables include knowledge of the intentions of other actors within the system, knowledge of the capabilities of other actors within the system and knowledge of the system rules. As in Easton's analysis, Kaplan's discussion shows an emphasis on the significance of information as a variable for describing the activities within political systems. In summary, when Kaplan develops a model of a political system he defines a plurality of unit actors behaving according to a set of essential rules which are subject to change, possessing varying capabilities and varying information. Given this frame of reference, Kaplan has developed several models of international systems applicable to past, present and, perhaps, future configurations of international politics.

The classical model of international politics in the West is the "balance of power" model. In accordance with his five sets of variables, Kaplan gives a rigorous definition of the balance of power. In the balance of power model,

---

[39] Kaplan, *Macropolitics,* p. 213.

the only actors are nation states. Each nation state has the goal of maximizing its security and prefers a high probability of survival to a moderate probability for dominance over other actors or for the elimination of other actors from the system. There are no nuclear weapons in the balance of power system, but economic productivity sporadically increases and, therefore, all actors seek a margin of safety. There are at least five major nations in the classical balance of power system, and each state requires allies if it is to fulfill its goal of maximizing security. Summing up the six major characteristics of the balance of power system is the principle that a general identity exists between the short and long term interests of the actors involved in a classical balance of power system. Each of the six characteristics function to support this principle. The fact that there are at least five major nations in the classical balance of power system makes it unlikely that any one nation will seek to impose dominance over another actor. The fact that allies are necessary to the maximization of security also tends to moderate the behavior of any single nation. Further, the absence of nuclear weapons constitutes some limit to the disruption that can be caused by military activity, and the sporadic character of economic advance decreases the chance that any one actor will permanently gain overwhelming capacities. While the classical balance of power model has provided the base point for the study of international politics in the West, it is no longer a good predictor of patterns of international relations. Kaplan has introduced several new models to describe the essential features of systems in which nuclear weapons, super-powers, international actors and lessened uncertainty about productivity appear. In the loose bipolar model there are contending blocs, neutrals, universal actors in the form of international organizations and nuclear weapons. In the tight bipolar system there are neither nonbloc members nor universal actors. Kaplan has also described hierarchical universal systems, a unit veto system, a very loose bipolar system, a détente system, an unstable bloc system and an incomplete nuclear diffusion system, of which the essential features can be grasped from the name. Each of these systems represents a way of describing the essential features of the present pattern of international politics, or a way of projecting future developments. None of Kaplan's models, with the possible exception of the classical balance of power model, gives full specification to the essential rules, the actor classificatory variables, the capability variables and the information variables. The loose bipolar model is a sketch of the system of international politics in the 1950s, while the tight bipolar system is a description of a more simplified two-power system which is, perhaps, useful for analytic purposes. In line with Kaplan's doubts about the advisability of conceptualizing changes in essential rules, these models do not specify principles of transformation. Thus, in his descriptions of various concrete models of international politics, Kaplan departs from the rigorous analytic categories of system type, system process and key sets of variables that he introduced in his discussion of general theory. There is a loose fit between the definitions of ultrastable and multistable systems and the descriptions of the classical balance of power and the loose bipolar systems. This gap between analytic categories and specific descriptions has been a recurrent difficulty for systems theorists of political life. While it does not destroy the value of systems theories as conceptual responses to general questions, or as imaginative perspectives on political existence, it does detract from the strictly scientific value of these theories.

Imaginative Perspective

Much more clearly than Easton does, Kaplan articulates the human perspective implicit in his theory. He states that from an abstract point of view human beings are "instrumental for maintaining the existence and interests of the political system."[40] However, Kaplan does not expect the human being as political actor to take the abstract point of view. From the viewpoint of "ultrastable individual human beings, the political system has value only as an instrument for implementing human values."[41] While the individual may or may not take the needs of the system into account when he is planning his action, there is no logical or theoretical reason why his interests should be subordinated to those of the political system. In fact, even political officials are not morally obligated to act in accordance with legally prescribed policy in all cases. The "myth that administrators have no responsibility except to carry out legally prescribed national policy has been responsible for some of the most sordid violations of individual values in the history of mankind."[42]

The fact that individuals need not serve the purposes of the political system gives rise to tragic dilemmas. Men are torn between the conflicting needs of adjusting to their unique personal situations and adjusting to the needs that are general to their communities. The only escape from this dilemma is to modify the environment "in such a way that the two sets of needs cease to be irreconcilable."[43] This ideal of harmony between individual and social requirements is present in the writings of Hegel, Marx and Dewey. Kaplan does not recommend that we sacrifice ourselves for the maintenance of the political system, or that we sacrifice the needs of the community for our own benefit. Instead, he suggests that we strive to bring system requirements into line with the satisfaction of human needs. Again, systems theorists need not idolize the political system. In fact, they may wish to change it to accord with the deepest human desires.

---

[40] Kaplan, *Macropolitics*, p. 178.
[41] Kaplan, *Macropolitics*, p. 179.
[42] Kaplan, *Macropolitics*, p. 178.
[43] Kaplan, *Macropolitics*, p. 167.

Karl W. Deutsch

Karl W. Deutsch has approached the analysis of political systems from the point of view of cybernetics. Cybernetics, which is the study of the methods of control and communication in living, mechanical and social systems, provides concepts that parallel many of the notions of everyday political discourse. In political life discussions of information, communication, control of behavior and command occur frequently. Deutsch has argued that the science describing the most general features of communication can aid us in placing our knowledge of political communication into a context and help us derive new relationships in the political world. Cybernetics has become an important intellectual current in the contemporary world due to the increasing development and use of electronic computers which can perform sophisticated operations on information and control complex mechanical processes. Theorists who apply the concepts of cybernetics to the description of political affairs suggest that many of the operations of computers are analogous to the decision-making processes of politics. Since computers are more readily understood than political systems, because they can be taken apart, analyzed, reconstructed and manipulated with facility, theorists like Deutsch contend that some of the implications of cybernetics can point to new areas of political study. Deutsch's work has reflected his interest in communication. His *Nationalism and Social Communication* suggested that the phenomenon of nationalism could best be interpreted through an analysis of the scope and intensity of communication within and between groups.[44] In *The Nerves of Government* Deutsch generalized his work on nationalism to the level of a general theory of politics.[45] Since the publication of *The Nerves of Government* Deutsch has conducted studies and has written theoretical essays about the processes of political integration.[46] Our discussion will be concerned mainly with the concepts elaborated in *The Nerves of Government*.

The Political Question

Like Easton, Deutsch has been concerned with clearly defining a set of questions for empirical political analysis and describing a scope for political study wider than the analysis of power. Deutsch argues that power is "neither the center nor the essence of politics."[47] Power, or the ability of an individ-

---

[44] Karl W. Deutsch, *Nationalism and Social Communication* (Cambridge: MIT Technology Press, 1953).

[45] Karl W. Deutsch, *The Nerves of Government* (New York: The Free Press, 1966).

[46] Philip E. Jacob and James V. Toscano (eds.), *The Integration of Political Communities* (Philadelphia: J. B. Lippincott Co., 1964).

[47] Deutsch, *The Nerves*, p. 124.

ual or an organization to "act out" its character, is merely one of the "currencies" of politics, a means of having actions performed to maintain stability or attain a goal. Other political currencies are influence, force, voluntary coordination and the trading of favors. None of these currencies can define politics because they constitute alternative means to fulfilling the essence of politics. Together they define political processes, but not the meaning of these processes. Thus, all of the currencies are secondary to the essence of politics, which is the "dependable coordination of human efforts and expectations for the attainment of the goals of the society."[48] Deutsch derives from cybernetics the definition of politics as the coordination of human activity for the fulfillment of social goals. He contends that while many studies of political affairs have concentrated on power, or the enforcement of commands, information must precede compulsion.[49] In other words, before a command can be given or an action can be compelled the commander must know how to transmit his message to the subordinate and have it understood. Further, no action can be compelled if the commander does not know how to contact the subordinate. Deutsch also argues that "information must precede compliance."[50] One cannot follow an order that he neither receives nor understands. It is on these grounds that Deutsch maintains that political theorists should seek to understand the coordination of human activity rather than who gets what, when and how. Deutsch's and Easton's definitions of politics can be compared. Both writers attempt to provide a scope for political study that includes the analysis of power as well as topics that logically precede it. Easton argues that the question of who gets what, when and how implies a process through which values are allocated and rules regulate the competition for scarce values. Deutsch contends that the question of who gets what, when and how implies the possibility of information on what is available and how to get it. Both writers seem to be correct, but Deutsch appears to be correct only in a trivial sense. While it is important to recognize that political conflicts are usually mediated through cultural norms, it is no great insight to realize that political activity depends upon communication. All interpersonal relations depend upon communication in much the same way and Deutsch's argument does not allow him to distinguish politics from any other human activity. Further, information gathering may be a primary political problem for someone who already has significant resources of power. This person will want to know how he can exercise his power most effectively. However, for the person with little power information may not be very useful. Gaining resources of power will be this person's problem.

---

[48] Deutsch, *The Nerves*, p. 124.
[49] Deutsch, *The Nerves*, p. 151.
[50] Deutsch, *The Nerves*, p. 152.

Deutsch's guiding questions for political analysis flow from his definition of politics as the coordination of human efforts and expectations for the attainment of the goals of the society. From the concepts of cybernetics he derives four questions. First, he asks, "... what is the *load* upon the political decision system of the state?"[51] By this he means, what is the amount and rate of change with which the government must cope? The concept of load is similar to Easton's notion of stress. Second, he asks, "What is the *lag* in the response of a government ... to a new emergency or challenge?"[52] Third, he asks, "What is the *gain* of the response—that is, the speed and size of the reaction of a political system to new data it has accepted?"[53] Finally, he asks, "What is the amount of *lead*, that is, of the capability of a government to predict and to anticipate new problems effectively?"[54] Deutsch's approach is similar to Easton's in that it fixes attention on the adaptation of a political system to change. However, it differs from Easton's analysis because it does not specify any basic political objects. For Deutsch, political systems represent means of solving community problems and they may undergo drastic internal rearrangement as problems change. Deutsch is even more impressed with the possibilities for adaptation and creativity in social systems than is Easton. In their attempts to account for change within their theories both Easton and Deutsch differ from Kaplan. If we wanted to summarize Deutsch's four guiding questions into one query, we might ask: How do political systems effect the coordination of human activity for the attainment of social goals in a world of change and emerging problems? It is in terms of such a question that Deutsch organizes his fundamental concepts.

The Fundamental Concepts

The basic concept in Deutsch's political theory is "self-modifying communications network" or "learning net." A learning net is "any system characterized by a relevant degree of organization, communication, and control, regardless of the particular processes by which its messages are transmitted and its functions carried out—whether by words between individuals in a social organization, or by nerve cells and hormones in a living body, or by electric signals in an electronic device."[55] The notion of a learning net shows the high level of generality made possible by cybernetics. Certain machines, organisms, human beings and social organizations can be described by the same term. All of these units are alike in that they are able to "steer" themselves, or adjust to disturbances in their environments as they pursue

---

[51] Deutsch, *The Nerves*, p. 189.
[52] Deutsch, *The Nerves*, p. 189.
[53] Deutsch, *The Nerves*, p. 190.
[54] Deutsch, *The Nerves*, p. 190.
[55] Deutsch, *The Nerves*, p. 80.

their goals. Thus, politics is a goal-seeking process that depends upon adequate response to feedback. Feedback is just as significant for Deutsch as it is for Easton. Goal-seeking processes are distinct from other mechanical processes in four ways. First, the goal sought is outside the goal-seeking system. Second, the system itself "is not isolated from its environment" but depends on information from the environment and from itself for effectiveness in goal attainment. This is another way of emphasizing the importance of feedback. Third, the goal may change. Fourth, a goal may be attained in various ways. This point emphasizes the difference between strategy and tactics that frequently appears in everyday political discourse. Those learning nets that are most successful in the process of steering themselves are likely to be flexible in tactics and relatively stable in strategy. The discussion of politics as a steering process and government as a steering mechanism points up a weakness in Deutsch's approach. Deutsch accepts the goals of political systems as givens that are not to be explained by political science. However, politics can be viewed as a goal setting as well as a goal attaining process. It is here that Deutsch's unwillingness to grant power primary importance weakens his theory. Toward what goals the political system is being steered cannot be explained by a description of the steering mechanism. It can be explained, perhaps, by a study of groups that have relatively high resources of power.

Learning nets have three basic elements: receptors, effectors and feedback controls. Receptors collect information from the environment, effectors execute decisions and feedback controls inform the system of the consequences of the decisions for goal attainment. Receptors, effectors and feedback controls provide learning nets with degrees of autonomy. Simple learning nets have autonomy because they have feedback controls. They can adapt to environmental disturbances without surrendering their goals by receiving, assimilating and adjusting to information from the environment. More complex learning nets like human beings and political systems can "change their goals, or 'reset' their feedbacks, by interactions with information from their past, stored in particular memory devices."[56] Autonomous systems must receive three types of information. First, they must receive information about their environments so that they can react to disturbances and take advantage of opportunities. Second, they must receive information from their pasts so that they can maintain their integrities. Third, they must receive information about themselves and their pasts so that they can maintain integration. The decisive point of decision making in a political system is the boundary between maintenance of patterns from the past and adaptive change to new circumstances. Any complex learning net encounters the central problem of steering a course between self-destruction through

---

[56] Deutsch, *The Nerves*, p. 128.

screening out information from the environment and self-dissolution through screening out information from the past. Without memory there is no autonomy and without adaptation there is no system. The ability of complex learning nets to recombine goals and even create new ones in response to opportunities and dangers in the environment thus gives rise to the continuous problem of steering a course between two poles of destruction.

Both individuals and political systems encounter the problem of autonomy. People frequently worry about the possibility that they have surrendered their personalities and characters through adapting to the wishes of others or through performing uncongenial social roles. Some of the worst nightmares of totalitarianism concern the destruction of memory and the enforced compliance to ever-changing directives. Conformity is often viewed as synonymous with loss of individuality and integrity. People also often worry about the possibility that they are slaves of their past, bound to routines and attitudes that have lost their meaning and relevance. When individuality finds no response in the environment the loneliness and despair of the isolated match the anxiety of the compulsive conformist. In the case of political systems the continuous conflict between liberal and conservative policies represents the dialogue implicit in the problem of autonomy. Conservatives charge that liberals wish to repudiate national memories and plunge the state into destructive adventures. Liberals respond that conservatives aim at freezing the state so that it will eventually be destroyed through maladaptation. It is not enough to counsel moderation. Depending on the goals sought, sometimes rapid and far-reaching change is necessary and sometimes it is prudent to stand pat. Deutsch counsels us to approach life and politics guided by the concept of grace: "The concept of grace may thus imply the treatment of the world beyond the self, or beyond any particular group or organization, as the potential source of aids or resources in goal-setting and learning."[57]

From the description of the central dilemma of a learning net as steering a course between self-destruction through screening out information from the environment and self-dissolution through screening out information from the past, Deutsch derives a set of subsidiary political dilemmas. Given the principle that every self-governing system must remake its own memories and inner structure as it acts, Deutsch lists five ways in which systems can fail. First, a decision system can fail through loss of power. It can be unable to mobilize the resources and energies necessary for attaining goals. Second, systems can fail through loss of intake. Systems which dissolve through loss of intake are unable to gather and order the information necessary for attaining goals. Here, the receptors of the systems in question have failed to function adequately. The systems in question do not have the information which would enable them to identify obstacles in the way of attaining goals and

---

[57] Deutsch, *The Nerves*, p. 237.

thereby avoid or surmount them. Third, systems can fail through loss of steering capacity. Here, the effectors of the systems in question have failed to function adequately. The systems in question cannot integrate the information presented them by the receptors into a policy and then put that policy into action. A concrete example of failure of effectors is the breakdown of a multi-party parliamentary system through the inability of the various factions to agree upon a governing coalition. In this case, there may be adequate information about the environment, but no way of using that information to develop and apply plans of action. Fourth, a political system can fail through loss of depth of memory. Here, the system is unable to mobilize the lessons of past experience in its efforts to steer a course toward goals. The loss of depth of memory describes the situation in which the tension between screening out information from the environment and screening out information from the past that characterizes autonomy is destroyed through completely screening out past experience. Loss of intake, of course, describes the situation in which this tension is destroyed through completely screening out information from the environment. Thus, the causes of system failure can be related to the central dilemma of autonomy. Fifth, a political system can fail through loss of capacity for partial inner rearrangement. Here, the system is so inflexible that it is unable to change even the subsidiary decision-making procedures in response to environmental disturbances. In Easton's terms, failure through loss of capacity for partial inner rearrangement would mean that neither the authorities nor the minor aspects of the regime were amenable to change. The system that cannot reform itself will be characterized eventually by failure of receptors, effectors or feedback controls. Inability to undertake partial inner rearrangement is primarily a problem of feedback controls. Sixth, a political system can fail through loss of capacity for comprehensive or fundamental rearrangement of inner structure. Here, the system is inflexible in the sense that it is unable to change primary decision-making procedures in response to environmental disturbances. Following Easton again, failure through loss of capacity for comprehensive or fundamental rearrangement would mean that neither the major aspects of the regime nor the political community were amenable to change. Under certain conditions, the system that cannot revolutionize itself will be characterized by failure of receptors, effectors or feedback controls. As in the case of failure through loss of capacity for partial inner rearrangement, failure through loss of capacity for self-revolution is primarily a problem of feedback controls. Loss of power, loss of intake, loss of steering capacity, loss of depth of memory, loss of capacity for partial rearrangement or reform of inner structure and loss of capacity for comprehensive or fundamental rearrangement of inner structure exhaust Deutsch's list of the ways in which systems can fail.

These modes of system failure are related to the three basic elements of learning nets: receptors, effectors and feedback controls. Loss of power and loss of steering capacity define the failure of effectors, loss of intake and loss of depth of memory define the failure of receptors, and loss of capacity for partial inner rearrangement of structure and loss of capacity for comprehensive or fundamental rearrangement of inner structure define the failure of feedback controls. The modes of system failure are also closely connected to the central dilemma of a learning net: steering a course between self-destruction through screening out information from the environment and self-dissolution through screening out information from the past. In effect, when systems fail they have destroyed the tension between the two poles of the dilemma and have eliminated one type of information. In the most straightforward sense, loss of intake describes screening out information from the environment and loss of depth of memory describes screening out information from the past. However, lack of capacities for reform of self-revolution are also conditioned by the failures to learn from experience and' expand the range and depth of present experience. Loss of power and loss of steering capacity are equally tied to the way systems adjust to the central dilemma. Loss of power may come about through the failure to recognize opportunities in the environment and loss of steering capacity may eventuate through the failure to recognize obstacles in the environment. Thus, the analysis of the modes of system failure illuminates the categories of Deutsch's general theory.

Deutsch relates his discussion of the modes of system failure to traditional conceptions of human sin. Loss of power corresponds to the sin of over-valuing the present over the future, loss of intake corresponds to the sin of overvaluing memories over current experiences, loss of steering capacity corresponds to the sin of overvaluing structure over function, loss of depth of memory corresponds to the sin of overvaluing established routines for recalling and recombining data over new ways of exploiting the stock of past experiences, and loss of the capacities for partial inner rearrangement of structure and comprehensive or fundamental rearrangement of inner structure corresponds to the sin of overvaluing specific commitments over the realization of long-term goals. Deutsch summarizes the essential elements of system failure and sin in a single principle: "They involved overestimation or over-valuation of the organization compared to its environment, or its past methods and commitments over new ones, and of its current will and inner structure over all possibilities of fundamental change."[58]

For Deutsch, there are two primary orientations present in every human organization. First, there is the activity involved with fulfilling the goals that provide the organization with its reason for existence. Second, there is the activity involved with maintaining the organization in such condition that it is able to steer a course toward attaining the stipulated goals. System failure and

---

[58] Deutsch, *The Nerves*, p. 229.

sin occur when the orientation comprising activities involved with maintaining the organization takes precedence over the orientation comprising activities involved with attaining stipulated goals. It is here that the concept of grace as treatment of the world beyond the self, or beyond any particular organization, as the potential source of aids or resources in goal-setting and learning becomes particularly important. Deutsch identifies three attitudes of grace. First, the individual or official should recognize that all routines will eventually become insufficient for the preservation of autonomy. Second, the individual or official should recognize that the universe contains essential data for the solution of problems involved in goal attainment which has not yet been discovered. Third, the individual or official should become receptive to new experiences and be prepared to commit the structures of his personality and his organizations to significant change when the experiences warrant such a course. Deutsch concludes with the remark that his communications theory of political existence has the final purpose of increasing the opportunities for constructively adaptive behavior in human life: "All studies of politics and all techniques and models suggested as instruments of political analysis have this purpose: that men should be able to act in politics with their eyes open."[59]

Imaginative Perspective

Karl Deutsch has developed an imaginative perspective on the political world and its possibilities. Like Kaplan he is in the classical tradition of political thought and does not shun discussions of political values. He has stated that a mature theory of politics "should help us to identify viable, growing, and creative patterns of political values and political action."[60] While Deutsch's definition of politics as the process of steering a course toward the realization of given values does not include a judgment on which values are the most desirable, Deutsch does make such a judgment within his theory. The key political value for Deutsch is the capacity for integrative behavior. By this he means the ability of human organizations to harmonize several levels of autonomous systems and enhance the self-determination and autonomous growth of individuals.[61] In accordance with this vision Deutsch has defined the basic human right as the right of every person "to learn at his own speed with his own inner equipment, in an unbroken sequence of autonomous acts of learning, in which his own unique stored past and his own acquired preferences at every single step have at least some share in the outcome."[62] Deutsch's vision of the political good stands as evidence that a theory grounded in the concepts of cybernetics can be consistent with a moral

---

[59] Deutsch, *The Nerves*, p. 255.
[60] Deutsch, *The Nerves*, p. xxvi.
[61] Deutsch, *The Nerves*, p. 253.
[62] Deutsch, *The Nerves*, p. 132.

humanism. However, this humanism is only partial in that it slights material and structural preconditions for human dignity. This partiality is also a consequence of grounding a political theory in cybernetics. Perhaps a more adequate political morality would take the form of a synthesis of a theory of human needs like Kaplan's and a theory of development through learning.

Theories
of
Political
Subsystems

3

Political activities can be described in terms of smaller units than entire political systems. While a study of the entire political system has the advantage of comprehensiveness and appropriateness to the problem of order, the analysis of smaller units can aid in understanding better the stresses that political systems undergo. Normally our actions are not directly relevant to the political system. Rather, in great part our political activities and our political understanding are mediated through the groups, organizations and roles in which we participate. Some political theorists have interpreted such groups, organizations and role networks as the primary actors in contemporary politics. This does not mean that groups, organizations and interrelated sets of rights and duties have the capacities for conscious thought, feeling and evaluation. Instead, these theorists are impressed by the fact that human activities are organized into collectivities that have consequences for the affairs of the entire society. As in the case of systems theories of politics, the basis of theories of political subsystems is the notion of a meaningful cross section of activity. Concrete human beings are not organized into functioning collectivities. Specific human activities are organized.

There are three major foci of theories of political subsystems. Theorists of subsystems can concentrate their attention on the activities of interest groups, formal organizations or role networks. These concentrations of interest are not mutually exclusive. Rather, they are consistent with one another and perhaps supplementary. Despite differences in language, theories of political subsystems are quite similar in content, just as theories of political systems closely resemble one another. Further, like theories of the political system, theories of political subsystems are usually responses to the problem of order. The two kinds of theories differ from one another primarily in point of view. Theorists of the political system evaluate the consequences of organized cross sections of human activity for the persistence of the entire political system, while theorists of political subsystems evaluate the consequences of organized cross sections of human activities for the persistence of the patterns of relations between such organizations and for the persistence of the organizations themselves. The various theories of political subsystems can be classified in terms of similar distinctions of points of view. Interest group theorists mainly study those meaningful cross sections of activity involving demands that groups make upon one another in a society. Theorists of formal organization study the ways decisions are made or values are allocated in the bureaucracies that characterize contemporary life. As a summary statement one may say that interest group theorists are primarily concerned with relations between groups and theorists of formal organization are mainly interested in relations within groups. Interest groups considered as patterns of interaction among members are organizations. Organizations making demands upon other groups and organizations are interest groups. Role theorists study the rights and duties, expectations and behaviors that cluster around a human activity. Political systems, interest groups and formal organizations can be viewed as sets of roles. However, the subsystem that role theorists primarily study is the role network rather than the interest group or the formal organization. Role networks are organized around culturally defined human activities. An example of a network of political roles would be the set of roles clustered about the activity of representation. The role network defining representation would include the rights and duties, expectations and behaviors associated with the cross sections of activity called representative, constituent, lobbyist, legislator, journalist, political letter writer, among other culturally defined activities. Interest groups and organizations often formalize roles and organize them around purposes. Thus, interest group theories, organization theories and role theories appear to supplement one another.

Whenever we act politically we are participants in the political system. This is an analytic statement, true by virtue of the definition of the political system as the meaningful cross section of human activity that is called political. However, the cross section of human activity called "political" can be further differentiated into kinds of activity such as representative activity and administrative activity. Whenever we act politically we participate in a certain kind of political activity. Thus, whenever we act politically we are participants in a political subsystem. This is not merely an exercise in definition. Our discussion points to the fact that most of the time we do not have an image of the entire political system in mind when we act. Rather, we act politically with reference to one of the interest groups, organizations or role systems that forms a part of the political system. Thus, we are often unaware of the consequences that our actions have for other groups, organizations, role systems, individuals, and for the political system as a whole.

The Political Questions

Like systems theories of politics, theories of political subsystems were developed as responses to the problem of order. Each type of theory of the political subsystem poses the problem of order and responds to it from its own special point of view. The general problem of order as it is expressed by David Easton—How do political systems persist through change?—can be restated in many contexts. From the perspective of interest group theory the problem of order is expressed as the query, How do political systems persist when groups continually demand actions and resources from one another? Political interest groups make demands for authoritative allocations of values in the political system. In the terms of Easton's systems theory, they are the source of demands on the political system and, therefore, the source of stress. Thus, the interest group theory proposed by David Truman is consistent with the systems theory of David Easton. Both theories are responses to the problem of order, and both theories are concerned with the persistence of the entire political system.

Unlike theories of political interest groups, theories of formal organizations are not primarily concerned with accounting for the persistence of the entire political system. Instead, these theories pose the question, How do subsystems persist under stress? A single organization can be considered as a quasi-political system. Organizations have systems of authority, demands are made upon them, supports are given them and they produce outputs. The concept of feedback can be applied to organizations because the consequences of their outputs affect the adjustment of their patterns of decision making. Just as in the case of theories of the political system, various verbal formulations of the problem of order have been worked out for organizational subsystems. For Herbert Simon, the problem of order is phrased in terms of the question of how the choices of human beings are restricted so that they can undertake cooperative action. Thus, the organization is a container in which only certain actions are possible. From another point of view, the organization provides an environment for choice by limiting factors that a decision maker must take into account when he is confronted with a choice. For Peter Blau, the problem of order requires inquiry into how complex patterns of social relations become organized out of simple processes of relation between human beings. Blau argues that the organization is a system of exchanges. Power relations arise from one's surrender of his power of decision in return for other goods. Simon's theory of decision making and Blau's theory of exchange are very similar.

While interest group theories describe the entire political system from the viewpoint of the units that press demands and provide supports, and organization theories view organizations as quasi-political systems with their own "life-processes" and their own requirements of coping with stress, role theories pose the problem of order in terms of discovering how social relations become predictable. For Heinz Eulau, roles, or patterns of culturally defined rights and duties, social expectations of behavior and personal premises of choice, provide the predictability that makes human relations possible. Eulau views political behavior as defined by role networks, and deemphasizes interest groups and organizations in favor of the more general concept of culturally defined, or discriminable activities. Yet he still defines the problem of the political theorist as one of accounting for how order arises from a hypothetical chaos. For Eulau, as for the other theorists of the political system and political subsystems, social life is possible because standardized norms and values are known, supported and observed. Whether it is a political drama in which we have a part (Eulau) or a political game that we play (Truman), the plot or the rules are culturally defined and are altered drastically only at the peril of disturbing predictable social relations.

The Imaginative Perspective of Systems Approaches

For theorists of the political system and political subsystems, politics does not absorb all of a person's life. Political activity is merely one phase of human experience, one activity among many others. Truman epitomizes the perspective of theorists who adopt the systems framework when he discusses politics in terms of the pressing of demands by social groups upon one another. Politics is primarily a liaison activity. When any activity is being carried out without the accompaniment of frustration politics is superfluous. As soon as frustration appears political activities become possible, though not necessary. We may illustrate the conditions for politics implicit in systems theories with an example. Suppose one is absorbed in the activity of study and study is interrupted. The person experiences frustration and searches for a way to continue the activity. If the interruption is due to eye strain the person will either be forced to abstain from study for a time or use some medical aid to restore his vision. In either case frustration does not result in political activity. However, suppose the person knows that eye drops are available to restore his vision and he is prevented from obtaining or using them by other people. In this case he may demand access to eye drops, press a claim upon others. If he presses his claim so that it becomes a demand for an authoritative allocation of values he acts politically. In the case of the eye drops, he may demand a law or policy that eye drops be made available to people in his situation. Thus, he becomes a participant in the political system. As demander he is a liaison between the activity of study and the activity of authoritatively allocating values for a society. When societies become complex enough specialized roles for liaisons are developed. In large formal organizations such specialized roles also proliferate.

From the viewpoint of theorists of the political system and political subsystems, politics is an activity of transforming private problems into public problems. One experiences a frustration and demands that the entire society remove the barriers to the successful continuation of his activity. Thus, political systems are experiments in problem solving. As libraries are used for study, political systems are used to remove frustrations. However, just as librarians are sometimes so concerned with the preservation of books that they inordinately restrict their use and defeat the purposes of study, political authorities sometimes become so interested in the maintenance of forms of decision making that they restrict their use and defeat the purposes of removing frustrations. This implies that within the discussions of theorists of the political system and political subsystems there is a meaning of political activity for the human being. From the viewpoint of the political system or the political subsystem the outputs that flow from the processing of demands and supports are ethically neutral. From the viewpoint of the human being involved in political activity they may be of decisive importance. If politics arises as a means of overcoming frustration, political systems can function more or less effectively in eliminating barriers to activity. The individual human being as bearer of the desire to continue activity without frustration has an interest in having the political system produce outputs that are satisfactory to him. The individual as a human being has an obligation to aid in the creation of a political system that functions with maximum effectiveness to eliminate barriers to satisfying activity. This statement of obligation is not implied in the theories of the political system that we have discussed and the theories of political subsystems that we will analyze. As long as the human nature described by systems oriented theorists stresses diffuse desire rather than a structure of values as the primary motivating force in behavior, there can be no convincing statements of obligation. Most of the theorists of political systems and subsystems hold that there is no structure to human experience beyond that provided by cultural norms and values. This prevents such theorists from viewing politics as any more than a means to removing personal frustrations. The political system is an arena where private demands are processed. Public activity, based on one's status as a human being presupposes a structure to being human. Most current political theorists have stopped short of providing such a structure. Perhaps this is why they evaluate the consequences of political activities in terms of their effects on the persistence of the political system. The imaginative perspective of theorists of the political system and political subsystems is not devoid of human interest. It provides a basis for interpreting concrete political life and part of a foundation for public action.

David B. Truman

David B. Truman is the most important contemporary exponent of interest group theories of politics in the United States. His *The Governmental Process,* published in 1951, represents one of the first ambitious efforts in empirical theory influenced by the behavioral approach to the study of politics.[1] This book was an early attempt to synthesize concepts from sociology and anthropology, and concepts from a theory of political groups that had been developed early in the twentieth century. The combination of elements of Arthur Bentley's theory of the group process and concepts from related social sciences that makes up the theoretical portion of Truman's work was a vital strain in the behavioral movement until systems theories of politics became dominant in the mid-1960s.[2] However, the theories of the political system that we discussed in the preceding chapter do not constitute a repudiation of the kind of theorizing that Truman undertook. Rather, they can be viewed as efforts to generalize the first generation of behavioral theories beyond the boundaries of politics in the United States. While Truman claims that his group theory of politics can be applied effectively across cultures, almost all of his illustrative material concerns American politics. He is also interested in accounting for the kind of representative democracy that has appeared in the United States. Easton, Kaplan and Deutsch are more abstract than Truman and they are not as interested in the particular problems of American politics. Since the publication of *The Governmental Process,* Truman has done further work on the American political system.[3] In our discussion we shall be concerned with the questions, concepts and perspectives developed in *The Governmental Process.*

The Political Question

Truman is clear about the questions that he would like to answer in his analysis of political groups. He asks two general questions: "How can we account for the existence of a going and generally accepted polity in a context of diverse interest groups? Under what circumstances can one appropriately view with alarm the growth and activity of political interest groups?"[4] The first question is not very different from the queries posed by the theorists of the political system, although it is phrased in another vocabulary. Like

---

[1] David B. Truman, *The Governmental Process* (New York: Alfred A. Knopf, 1951).
[2] Arthur F. Bentley, *The Process of Government* (Chicago: University of Chicago Press, 1908).
[3] David B. Truman, "The American System in Crisis," *Political Science Quarterly* (December, 1959), pp. 481-97.
[4] Truman, *The Governmental Process,* p. xi.

Easton, Truman is impressed by the fact that relatively stable patterns of political decision making are maintained in many societies through a multitude of conflicts. He would like to understand how such persistence of patterns is possible. The differences in wording between Truman's first question and Easton's query—How do political systems persist through change?—show the issues involved in developing a technical vocabulary for political theory. If Truman's question, phrased in traditional language, is essentially the same as Easton's, why was it necessary for Easton to use the unfamiliar vocabulary of systems analysis? A close look at the wording of Truman's first question will reveal a good deal of imprecision. The key term in Truman's question is "polity." However, nowhere in *The Governmental Process* does Truman define this term. This is not merely a petty consideration. Unless we are clear about the meaning of "polity" we will not be able to develop any criteria for determining whether or not a polity is "going and generally accepted." Traditionally, polity has meant the constitution, or the most fundamental rules and practices, of a government or other organization. This is probably what Truman meant by the term. However, his lack of precision on this point distinguishes Truman from Easton. Easton was so concerned with defining the term "political system" because he understood that only by specifying the essential features of what persists could one determine the conditions, or even the fact, of its persistence.

Related to the vagueness of the term polity is the imprecision of the adjectival phrase "going and generally accepted." In Easton's discussion of the political system we know that we are concerned with the problem of understanding the persistence of processes for authoritatively allocating values for a society. No such knowledge is contained in the notion of a "going and generally accepted polity." This does not mean that Easton's definition of the political system is fully acceptable. We have already noted that Easton's discussion contains an ambiguity between the notions of power and formal authority. The point at issue is why theorists of the political system found it necessary to develop a technical vocabulary. It should now be clear that the language of systems theory is used for the purpose of furthering precision. In the succeeding discussion of Truman's theory we will assume that the major question is accounting for the persistence of the fundamental rules and practices that define the authoritative allocation of values in a society.

The third aspect of Truman's question concerns the meaning of the term "interest group." The distinctive unit of political analysis in Truman's theory is the interest group. This perspective gives Truman's theory a different emphasis from Easton's analysis. Easton's use of the political system itself as the fundamental unit of political analysis led him to stress factors making for consensus. Truman's use of a part of the political system as the basic unit in his analysis leads him to place more of a stress on the processes of conflict. This distinction between the concerns of systems theories and interest group theories does not reflect a fundamental logical difference between the two types of theories. Truman's interest group perspective is essentially a way of looking at the processes in the political system from the viewpoint of the demands made upon it. Interest groups may be defined provisionally as the relevant units that make demands for authoritative allocations of values in a society. Thus, Truman's first question can be rephrased in the language of systems theory: How do political systems persist in an environment of intense and conflicting demands made by interest groups? To focus one's analysis on a part of the political system does not imply that one rejects the concept of a political system. Truman's use of the term "polity" implies that the political system is a unit of theoretical analysis. Similarly, to fix one's attention on the political system as a whole does not imply that one rejects the importance of parts of the system or its subsystems. Easton's analysis of demands implies units that make the demands. These units are Truman's interest groups.

A full understanding of Truman's first political question will be furthered by an appreciation of precisely what he means by the term "interest group." Truman begins his discussion by observing that human beings are always found in associations or groups. The idea of classical individualism, that individual human beings could be analyzed apart from their relations to one another, is repudiated by Truman. He claims that there is no "human nature" that can be described and analyzed by isolating the individual from others. He postulates that people become "characteristically human" only in their group life.[5] Thus, the various attitudes and actions characteristic of different individuals in a given society will vary "according to the clusters of group affiliations that the individuals have."[6] From earliest childhood people attempt to become accepted participants in the groups to which they have access. The specific groups in which people interact are a major determinant of the contents of their judgments of fact and value. Therefore, like Easton, Truman interprets the task of political science as the analysis of cross sections of human activity. Interest group theory by-passes the problem of describing the individual personality and the patterns of human choice by fixing attention on cross sections of activity that are shared by numbers of persons. Of course, any particular individual is involved in several groups. For the individual, the actions required by two or more of these groups may be mutually frustrating, or in conflict. The consequences of such frustration or conflict on the individual's personality are not a primary concern of interest group theorists.

---

[5] Truman, *The Governmental Process*, p. 15.
[6] Truman, *The Governmental Process*, p. 16..

Truman defines a group as a set of interactions or relationships that have a particular character. He notes that the interaction rather than the particular shared characteristic of group members is the crucial determinant of a group. He does not attempt to account for the specific kinds of interactions that occur in various societies, or to describe the types of interactions that occur in all societies. Truman does remark that the "complexity and variation of group life among human cultures apparently grew out of the daily activities of their participants and reflect the kinds of techniques that the cultures have developed for dealing with the environment."[7] Thus, Truman expects the particular pattern of group activities in a given society mainly to be a function of the level of technology attained in that society. While Truman is not explicitly a technological determinist, underlying his political theory is the collective encounter of human beings with an often hostile environment.

An interest group is a set of interactions or relationships that has a particular and definable character. Interest groups are distinguished from other groups by the condition that on "the basis of one or more shared attitudes" they make "certain claims upon other groups in the society for the establishment, maintenance, or enhancement of forms of behavior that are implied by the shared attitudes."[8] Out of the relations among people in groups arise relatively standardized ways of responding to events. Truman calls these responses norms or shared attitudes. These norms are essentially standards of judgment. They provide guidelines to the individual for determining what facts are relevant in a wide range of situations and for deciding what behavior is proper in a number of contexts. While new experiences and situations may eventually change the norms of a given group, at any particular time people who do not live up to the norms of the groups in which they participate are likely to be punished with the loss of some esteem, wealth or power. Group norms may be interpreted as the rules through which a group has attained an adjustment to its environment that permits its characteristic activities to continue. When this adjustment or equilibrium is disturbed, efforts are made to reestablish the equilibrium. All groups are interest groups in the sense that they are based on shared attitudes. All groups provide criteria for what facts are relevant in a range of situations and what behaviors are proper in those situations. For example, the members of a group of policemen controlling a riot are not likely to find the shapes of the rioters' ears relevant to their activities. Similarly, the norms of most police groups would prohibit members from lying down in the midst of a riot and dispassionately watching destruction go on.

However, interest groups are not defined merely by shared attitudes. In addition to the frames of reference common to all groups, interest groups are

---

[7]Truman, *The Governmental Process*, p. 26.
[8]Truman, *The Governmental Process*, p. 33.

defined by "shared attitudes toward what is needed or wanted in a given situation, observable as demands or claims upon other groups in the society."[9] These shared attitudes that are manifested as demands upon other groups Truman calls interests. Thus, an interest group is a set of relationships ordered around the prosecution of demands upon other groups. Demands made upon other groups in a society need not be political either in Easton's or Truman's terms. A labor union may make a demand upon a corporation for higher wages for its members without appealing for an authoritative allocation of values. In this case the labor union is an interest group but not a political interest group. For Truman, political interest groups arise when interest groups press their demands "through or upon any of the institutions of government."[10] As in the case of Truman's use of the term "polity," the term "government" is left undefined. We may assume that a working definition of "government" in the language of systems theory would be the set of processes through which demands are converted into binding allocations of values for a society. Thus, interest groups press demands on other groups in a society through the political system. It is now possible to understand how Truman's problem of accounting for the existence of a going and generally accepted polity in a context of diverse interest groups is a restatement of the problem of order. Truman is really asking, How do political systems persist under the stress of diverse and intense demands? Again, the problem of order can be viewed as the fundamental political question of current political theories.

Truman's second question—Under what circumstances can one appropriately view with alarm the growth and activity of political interest groups?—is less a question of empirical or descriptive political theory than it is a concern of normative or prescriptive theory. In order for one to "view with alarm" a political situation, one must hold some standard for identifying the good political life. Thus, it would not be enough to say that we could appropriately view with alarm any growth and activity of political interest groups that seriously threatened the persistence of the political system. A morally persuasive argument justifying this proposition would have to give good reasons for claiming that the persistence of any political system is always desirable or that the persistence of the particular political system under study is desirable. It is doubtful that a persuasive moral argument could be given justifying the persistence of any political system. Certainly, this is not what Truman intends when he poses his second question. Truman is interested in determining the conditions in which the growth and activity of political interest groups would imperil the survival of the kind of representative democracy present in the United States. He does not independently defend

---

[9] Truman, *The Governmental Process*, pp. 33-34.
[10] Truman, *The Governmental Process*, p. 37.

his preference for the American political system, but mixes his discussion of how political systems persist under the stress of diverse and intense demands with his concern for the survival of American political institutions. As a consequence of this method Truman sometimes limits the range of his theoretical generalizations to politics in the United States.

The Fundamental Concepts

Truman develops a set of concepts to answer his primary question, How can we account for the existence of a going and generally accepted polity in a context of diverse interest groups? These concepts can best be understood and related to one another if they are interpreted as extensions of the notion of interest groups. We recall that Truman held that the complexity and variation of group life among human cultures is mainly a function of the techniques that the cultures have developed in the encounter of human beings with their environment. During the last three hundred years in the West there has been a rapid growth in the sophistication and productive capacity of techniques for transforming the environment into goods and services to fulfill human wants. This growth is often referred to by the terms industrial revolution or scientific revolution. Truman states that the rapid development of industrial technologies has been the decisive element in modern history for explaining political affairs. For Truman the industrial revolution brought a new kind of society into being. With respect to political affairs, the primary impact of industrialization has been in intensifying the division of labor. The more intensive the division of labor, the more complex the society becomes and the more different kinds of activities are performed. Each particular activity has a set of attitudes associated with it. Thus, each particular activity can be viewed as the center of a group. Since any shared-attitude group can become an interest group, by increasing the variety of activities that are performed in a society industrialization also increases the possibilities for a multitude of interest groups to appear. For Truman the modern historical movement in political affairs has been an increase in the number of political interest groups.

Truman has developed a concept to account for the appearance of political interest groups. The "association" is a special kind of group that grows out of "tangent relations." Tangent relations tend to appear in complex societies characterized by intensive division of labor. In modern industrialized societies there are a multitude of groups representing the various activities that are performed in such societies. Since all individuals in a society participate in more than one activity, all individuals are members of more than one group. The groups in which an individual participates are "tangent" through the individual. Thus, a family group and a factory work group may be tangent to one another through a member of the family who works in the factory.

Tangency between groups may also exist through a "third group by which the tangent groups are similarly affected or through a common technique."[11] When the normal activities within two or more tangent groups are disturbed, the members are "likely to seek an adjustment through interaction with others in the tangent group, with whom they have 'something in common.' "[12] When a number of people have entered into the same kind of tangent relations and when they "interact with one another regularly on that basis" an association has appeared.[13] Particularly in the United States, examples of the appearance of associations are many and easily identifiable. For example, the occurrence of a war sets up tangent relations between the families of soldiers who have been taken as prisoners of war and the government that has imprisoned them. If the expectations of the families about the treatment of prisoners are disturbed by news reports of torture or poor conditions, or by the absence of information from or about the prisoners, the members of some families of prisoners are likely to attempt to have conditions improved or gain more information. If these people interact with one another by planning how to have conditions improved or how to gain information, and by acting on these plans, they have formed an association. If their activities involve making claims upon governmental groups for aid in alleviating the situation of prisoners their association has become a political interest group. According to Truman the more complex a society the more points of tangency there will be, the more likely disturbances will take place and the more likely political interest groups in the form of associations will arise. Truman summarizes his discussion of the association by stating that the "function of an association is to stabilize the relations of individuals in tangent groups."[14]

If associations function to stabilize the relations of individuals in tangent groups, a government is a set of activities and groups that functions "to establish and maintain a measure of order in the relationships among groups for various purposes."[15] This does not mean that the institutions of government function as an impartial arbiter, balancing the claims of the various political interest groups in accordance with a standard of the "public interest." Truman holds that there is no identifiable public interest against which conflicting claims can be judged. Various political interest groups phrase their demands in terms of a public interest so that they can maximize support. However, Truman claims that no activity, claim or demand is comprehensive enough to be in the public interest of a complex industrialized

---

[11] Truman, *The Governmental Process*, p. 40.
[12] Truman, *The Governmental Process*, p. 40.
[13] Truman, *The Governmental Process*, p. 40.
[14] Truman, *The Governmental Process*, p. 41.
[15] Truman, *The Governmental Process*, p. 45.

society. Therefore, governments represent various partial interests through their activities. Different governmental agencies may represent opposing interest groups, and governments can exclude the claims of some interest groups.

Since governments do not represent a public interest, the order that they establish in the relationships among groups is an order that favors some interest groups at the expense of others. Essentially, governmental policies reflect the purposes of interest groups that have gained effective access to governmental groups in which decisions that concern them are made. Truman states that the "common denominator" of the tactics of all interest groups is the attainment of "access to one or more key points of decision in the government."[16] Access is "the facilitating intermediate objective of political interest groups" that function to press claims on other groups in a society.[17] For an association, the typical kind of political interest group in a modern industrialized society, to have access to one or more key points of decision in the government, means that it can influence decisions in favor of the fulfillment of its demands. The history of interest group activities is the history of efforts to gain maximum access to the decision-making process; the process through which values are authoritatively allocated for a society. Truman states that the most important factor that affects the access that a group is likely to gain is "the position of the group or its spokesman in the social structure."[18] By this Truman means that the more esteem and wealth that a group and its members command the more power, as represented by access, that group will tend to have. Thus, when Truman claims that access is the facilitating intermediate objective of political interest groups he is making the point that individuals and groups normally attempt to improve their positions in the stratification system of a society.

If modern industrialized societies are characterized by a multitude of tangent relations that are the breeding grounds of interest groups, and if political interest groups are in a constant struggle to expand their access to the decision processes of government, Truman's first question becomes extremely important. How can we account for the existence of a going and generally accepted polity when we observe the stress generated by the continuous struggle among associations for access to the key points of decision in the government? How does the political system persist under such stress? Truman has provided two answers to this question. The first answer flows directly from his interpretation of interest groups as cross sections of activity. If each individual is the center of a large number of different activities, each individual is a member of a variety of groups. This does not

---

[16] Truman, *The Governmental Process*, p. 264.
[17] Truman, *The Governmental Process*, p. 264.
[18] Truman, *The Governmental Process*, p. 265.

mean that most people in a modern industrialized society are formal members of several associations, although many individuals do belong to one or more associations. It does mean that individuals are members of as many groups as their activities define. The situation described by the individual's participation in more than one group Truman calls "multiple membership." By itself, multiple membership does not guarantee the persistence of the political system. However, if we recall that an individual can be a member of groups that are in conflict, we will understand that membership in one group will sometimes counteract the effects of membership in a competing group. Truman observes that people subject to conflict because of their multiple memberships often withdraw from action in the conflict, or at least moderate their activities. Enough of such "overlapping membership" in competing groups tends to reduce the intensity of a conflict. Multiple membership makes it difficult for an individual to give his complete allegiance to any one group. For example, people usually do not absorb themselves completely in their work groups because they are also members of family groups. To follow an earlier example, members of an association concerned with the plight of war prisoners may not devote their full time to the group because of their family or job responsibilities. Overlapping membership tends to moderate the activities of any particular interest group. The group concerned with the war prisoner's situation might not resort to tactics like assassination of public officials because its members also participate in religious groups. Both multiple membership and overlapping membership tend to weaken the cohesion of political interest groups.

The second answer to the question—How can we account for the existence of a going and generally accepted polity when we observe the stress generated by the continuous struggle among associations for access to the key points of decision in the government?—depends upon the concept of a "potential group." For Truman, the fact that interest groups usually accept compromises is evidence that the political system is "not accounted for by the 'sum' of the organized interest groups in the society."[19] The interests in the norms and values that define constitutionalism, civil liberties and the generalized rules of proper political behavior within a society may not be organized into powerful associations, but they are an important influence on the conduct of many individuals in societies characterized by representative democracy. Truman calls these values and norms "rules of the game" and argues that they limit the means by which political interest groups seek access and the purposes for which access is used by such associations. Since the rules of the game represent widespread attitudes Truman says that they are "potential interest groups." By potential interest groups he means that although the rules of the game may not be defended by powerful associa-

---

[19] Truman, *The Governmental Process*, p. 51.

tions, if they are seriously breached by a political interest group or a governmental agency restorative actions will be taken. The probability that actions in defense of the rules of the game will be taken defines the potential interest groups. This is another way of saying that potential interest groups represent widely shared attitudes. Truman's rules of the game and potential groups are like Easton's "norms." Political systems persist through stress because norms effectively limit the content of demands and the ways in which demands are pressed. Not only does Truman ask the same question as the theorists of the political system; he also provides essentially the same answer. Current political theories do not resolve the problem of order by calling upon the individual's fear of punishment or his rationality. The controls that maintain social order are within the human being. They are put there in the process of socialization.

Imaginative Perspective

The vision of the political world from Truman's perspective is harsh. To gain a measure of predictability in his life while avoiding severe oppression the individual must accept two consequences. First, one must accept the consequence of division within the self and the conflict that follows from it. In Truman's political world groups are the effective actors. Individuals, as centers of many and often conflicting activities, are probably incapable of attaining consistent ways of life. However, although individuals are condemned to internal conflict, their anguish represents a blessing in disguise. Multiple and overlapping memberships mean that the individual can be liberated from the control of any single group. Even if some conflict is inevitable, people in modern representative democracies have the freedom to choose among a wide range of alternative activities. Of course, in a context of cross-cutting interests, liberty may not bring happiness to the free man. The second consequence that the individual must accept in Truman's political world is the necessity of compromise. One must give up any idea that he can identify what policies are in the public interest. He must treat his own demands as relative to the claims of others and be willing to negotiate a compromise in which all parties gain some satisfactions. This consequence only applies to people who accept the "rules of the game." Those who do not accept the rules of the game can presumably press their demands without limit. The division of the self and the politics of compromise have come under wide attack both within and outside of the discipline of political science. Many people demand the conditions for a consistent way of life. Many people also believe that there are some interests, like the interest in an environment free of pollution, that cannot be compromised. For Truman, demands for a life that minimizes conflict and demands that cannot be compromised are both utopian and dangerous. The good citizen defends the rules of the game and tolerates abrasion.

Herbert A. Simon

Herbert A. Simon was one of the first political theorists to apply to the field of public administration the concepts characteristic of the behavioral approach to the study of politics. As was the case with Truman's work, Simon's theoretical writings predate the time when empirical theorists became interested in systems theories of politics. However, parallel to our discussion of Truman's interest group theory, the concepts that Simon develops are consistent with the guiding themes of systems theories. Essentially, Simon is an organization theorist who attempts to develop general descriptions of the dynamics of public and private bureaucracies. Thus, instead of taking the entire political system as the area of his primary concern, Simon concentrates on the individual organization. In his *Administrative Behavior,* first published in 1947, Simon presented a theory of the operation of organizations based on the concept of decision making.[20] Since the end of World War II Simon has concentrated on extending and refining the ideas of *Administrative Behavior* by exploring mathematical models for his theoretical propositions. In *Models of Man* he collected a series of essays he had written on the mathematical models of human choice.[21] Despite his keen interest in descriptive theories, Simon has also attempted to devise ways in which governmental administrative organizations can be made more responsive to democratic values. He views the theory and practice of administration as closely linked to one another. In our discussion of Simon's theory of decision making in organizations we will be primarily concerned with the questions posed and the concepts developed in *Administrative Behavior.*

The Political Question

Herbert Kaufman has remarked that organization theory asks the same questions as general political theory.[22] For example, both political theorists and organization theorists have been occupied with the problem of coordination, or how the efforts of many human beings can be steered toward the fulfillment of collective goals. We have seen that this problem is central in the writings of Karl Deutsch. It is also important in Simon's theory of administrative decision making. Kaufman observes that the writings of both political theorists and organization theorists describe two processes by which coordination can be accomplished: "central direction, which means that the

---

[20] Herbert A. Simon, *Administrative Behavior* (New York: The Macmillan Company, 1960).

[21] Herbert A. Simon, *Models of Man* (New York: John Wiley and Sons, 1956).

[22] Herbert Kaufman, "Organization Theory and Political Theory," *American Political Science Review* (March, 1964), pp. 5-14.

activities of the elements of a system respond chiefly to cues and signals from some common source, and reciprocal relations, which means that the elements respond to cues and signals from each other."[23] Whether one is investigating the operation of an entire political system or the dynamics of a subsystem like an interest group or a government department, the processes of central direction and reciprocal relations will be present. Thus, theories of political systems and theories of human organizations do not answer different sets of questions. From the point of view of the organization theorist, the political system is merely one form of human organization that can be described in its most general features by the principles of organization theory. From the standpoint of the political theorist, administrative organizations are subsystems of the political system that can be described in some of their most general features by the principles of political theory. Of course, organization theorists do not confine themselves to posing the problem of coordination. Any question that is relevant to political theory can be rephrased in such a way that it will be relevant to organization theory.

Like Deutsch and Truman, Simon is careful to specify the questions that he is asking as his analysis proceeds. Throughout *Administrative Behavior* Simon restates his basic questions in different words, as if he wishes to exhaust the possible perspectives from which the study of organization can be seen. Thus, at one point he remarks that the "*central concern*" of administrative theory is with "*the boundary between the rational and the non-rational aspects of human behavior.*"[24] Here Simon is arguing that the description of the ways in which human choices are structured is the major task of the social sciences. He remarks that it is "with this problem—the process of choice which leads to action—that the present study is concerned."[25]

From another point of view Simon maintains that a "scientifically relevant description" of an organization would designate for "each person in the organization what decisions that person makes, and the influences to which he is subject in making each of these decisions."[26] Such a description would provide answers to what Simon has called the "big" questions of organization structure. Thus, the fundamental question that Simon poses is, How are decisions contained in organizations? Around this primary question are clustered a set of related queries. Simon finds a close relationship between the processes of decision making in an organization and the efficiency with which the organization realizes its goals. Thus, one of the subsidiary questions that he poses is, What are the "factors that determine the level of efficiency which is achieved by an administrative organization?"[27] Another question that is

---

[23] Kaufman, *American Political Science Review*, p. 7.
[24] Simon, *Administrative Behavior*, p. xxiv.
[25] Simon, *Administrative Behavior*, p. 1.
[26] Simon, *Administrative Behavior*, p. 37.
[27] Simon, *Administrative Behavior*, p. 38.

related to the problems of how decisions are contained and how organizations fulfill or fail to realize their goals, concerns the problem of how the efforts of many individuals are combined into an organizational plan. Why do people make decisions that further the attainment of organizational goals even when these decisions conflict with the realization of their personal values? The answer to this question is bound up with a consideration of the boundary between rational and nonrational behavior. Is there an organizational rationality apart from decisions that are in the interest of particular individuals? If one can talk intelligently in terms of such an organizational rationality, how are conflicts between organizational requirements and individual interests resolved? The problems of the structure and containment of decision making, organizational efficiency and the fit between organizational and personal goals can only be understood fully when the ideas of decision, efficiency and organizational goals are clarified. As in the case of our discussion of other current political theories, we will have to note the similarities and differences between Simon's language and the vocabularies of other political theorists.

As a first approximation to placing Simon's theory of administrative behavior in the context of current political theories, we may compare the questions that Simon poses to the queries advanced by other contemporary political theorists. With respect to the content of the fundamental political question, Simon has a different angle of vision than the other theorists. He is interested in describing the processes by which choices or decisions are limited in human societies. The force of this question can be assessed by exposing the problem out of which it arises. One can imagine a world in which, at every moment, each human being had the burden of choosing among all of the values that a person could attain and deciding among all of the possible means of attaining them. Nothing would be taken for granted in such a world and it is likely that no human purposes would be accomplished. At each moment one's plans would come under review and one would have to make a fresh decision about the way of life he wanted to attain and the means of realizing it. Existentialists like Sartre have argued that the person who lives in good faith must recognize that he faces just this situation. Sartre maintains that one can always revoke the projects to which he is committed and decide upon pursuing new ones. This does not mean that one would have to choose a new project or a new set of goals and means at every moment. It means that one would have to review his projects, goals and means continuously. Such continuous review would probably preclude extended and purposive actions. Human beings living in good faith would be in Hamlet's situation of constantly reviewing the motives and consequences of acts. Theorists like Simon are impressed by the fact that human beings do not live in a world in which they decide anew about the nature of their projects at every moment. They agree that the conditions for good faith described by Sartre are thinkable, but they observe that nobody meets these conditions and that very few people even approach fulfilling them. For human beings living within groups decisions are always limited by premises or assumptions that they take for granted. Simon holds that these premises or assumptions are expressed in the goals of social organizations and their authority structures. This does not mean that Simon believes that any given instance of the organizational containment of choice is good. He remarks that the "highest level of integration that man achieves consists in taking an existing set of institutions as one alternative and comparing it with other sets."[28] Like the existentialists Simon is concerned with the maximization of the values of freedom and responsibility. One way of attaining the maximization of these values is understanding the obstacles in the way of realizing the conditions necessary for good faith. By posing the problem of order in terms of how choices and decisions are contained in human societies, Simon has made his work relevant to concerns far beyond those of behavioral theory in political science.

While Simon's fundamental question is not similar to those of other major theorists in a straightforward sense, his emphasis on the way decisions are patterned in terms of organizational goals is similar to Deutsch's concern with government as a process of steering collective efforts toward social goals. Like Deutsch, Simon emphasizes the importance of communications processes in defining the kinds of decisions that are made in a system. Both Easton and Deutsch were impressed by the importance of the concept of information feedback for the social sciences. Similarly, Simon claims that cybernetics may represent "the real core of the new behavioral *Zeitgeist.* "[29] The centrality of communications processes in Simon's theory is suggested by one of his formulations of his basic question: "The question to be asked of any administrative process is: How does it influence the decisions of . . . individuals? Without communication, the answer must always be: It does not influence them at all."[30]

An understanding of the way in which decisions are contained in human organizations depends on clarification of the concept "decision." In the most general terms, a decision is a "conscious or unconscious selection of particular actions out of all those which are physically possible to the actor and to those persons over whom he exercises influence and authority."[31] Simon emphasizes the point that in his theory decisions are not necessarily conscious and deliberate. All organisms are continuously selecting stimuli from their environments to which they react by assimilation, rejection or transformation. The range of stimuli to which an organism will react need not be limited consciously. In the case of human beings habits unconsciously contain

---

[28] Simon, *Administrative Behavior,* p. 101.
[29] Simon, *Administrative Behavior,* p. xxix.
[30] Simon, *Administrative Behavior,* p. 108.
[31] Simon, *Administrative Behavior,* p. 3.

both the kinds of stimuli to which people respond and the ways that they respond to them. For example, in the early morning habit may constrain a person to respond to the visual stimulus of a coffee pot by filling it with water and placing it on the stove. The person does not think of why he is not responding to the visual stimulus of a plate that is next to the coffee pot, or why he has not responded to the stimulus of the coffee pot by placing it in the cupboard. By filling the coffee pot with water and placing it on the stove, the person has made a decision to select some actions from a wide range of physically possible actions. However, the person has not consciously deliberated about his action. He has performed it almost automatically. Perhaps at some time in the past the person had made a conscious decision that drinking coffee early in the morning was desirable and that the goal of drinking coffee could only be realized if, among other conditions, boiling water was available. Further, it is possible that the person thought about how water might be boiled in the least time at the least cost and with the least effort, and decided upon buying a certain kind of coffee pot. Each of these conscious decisions on ends and means later became habitual.

Whether or not a particular decision follows a process of conscious deliberation, it is based on premises of fact and value. For Simon, the basic unit of political analysis is not the decision, but the premise of the decision. A premise may be defined as a reason for making a decision. Value premises state that a certain situation is desirable, while factual premises state the conditions in which a desirable situation will come about. With reference to the example of drinking coffee in the early morning, a value premise is that drinking coffee is a desirable activity, while a factual premise is that a condition for having coffee to drink is boiling water. This does not mean that drinking coffee is a desirable activity according to a standard of value independent of the desires of a particular person. For Simon, a value premise states someone's preference for an activity or a state of affairs. Decisions in human organizations are contained by limits on the premises that provide the reasons, or grounds, for these decisions.

The Fundamental Concepts

We may recall that Simon holds that the central concern of administrative theory is with the boundary between the rational and the nonrational aspects of human behavior. In order to resolve his problem of how decisions, or choices, are limited in human organizations, Simon defines a standard of rational choice and then shows how organizations limit rationality. Simon views rationality as a process of selecting preferred alternatives from a range of possibilities, in accordance with a system of values that allows one to evaluate the consequences of the different possible behaviors. Thus, rational choice has several components. First, the rational decider must have a value system, or a set of goals that he wants to realize. He must be capable of ranking these goals in an order of preference so that he will be able to resolve conflicts among them. His list of priorities must be well defined enough so that he can compare them on a scale. Second, the rational decider must know the full range of possibilities for action. Further, he must know the consequences of each action for the realization of his goals. Third, the rational decider must be capable of applying the most efficient means to attaining his ends. Efficiency here means the application of those means which will produce the maximum realization of goals with a given expenditure of resources. When we say that the rational decider must be capable of applying the most efficient means to attaining his ends we do not mean that the most efficient possible means must be available to him. We only mean that he is psychologically capable of applying the most efficient means available *to him*, to the realization of his goals.

Simon calls the rational decider "economic man." Economic man confronts the world in all of its complexity and with all of its possibilities for action, and selects the "best alternative from among all those available to him."[32] Simon contrasts economic man with "administrative man" who realizes that he perceives a "drastically simplified model of the buzzing, blooming confusion that constitutes the real world," and selects an alternative that appears satisfactory.[33] While economic man maximizes the realization of his goals, administrative man "satisfices." Satisficing is a term coined by Simon that refers to behavior chosen in a situation in which the decider cannot fully rank his goals in order of preference, does not know the full range of possibilities for action, cannot predict the consequences of each action for the realization of his goals and is capable of applying means to ends. Thus, administrative man is economic man somewhat bewildered about his goals and lacking complete information about alternatives and their consequences. To the extent that administrative man is able to order his preferences and comprehend his possibilities for action he will approach the maximizing behavior of economic man. It is important to note that administrative man is not "irrational" in the sense that he will not act to realize his goals efficiently when he knows them and understands the means to reaching them. Simon implies that the irrational behavior characteristic of someone who is psychologically incapable of applying the appropriate means to attain his ends is not a proper subject for the organization theorist to study. Organization theory assumes that people will act to realize their preferences when they know them. Abnormal psychologists study the conditions for behavior that deviates from this standard. When administrative man satisfices he chooses a course of action that, in the face of incomplete information, he believes will aid in the realization of some of his goals.

Simon defines the limits of rationality as incompleteness of knowledge,

---

[32] Simon, *Administrative Behavior*, p. xxv.
[33] Simon, *Administrative Behavior*, p. xxv.

difficulties of anticipation and restrictions on the scope of behavior possibilities. Complete rationality requires that the decider know the consequences of each choice he makes for the fulfillment of his values. Such knowledge would be possible only in the context of a fully developed social science that could be used to predict with precision future states of social relations. Nothing close to this ideal social science exists at the present time, and people must act with uncertainty about the ultimate results of their decisions. Complete rationality also requires that the decider anticipate the satisfaction that he will derive from a future state of affairs. It is nearly impossible for a human being to evaluate an anticipation in the same way that he evaluates an experience. Here Simon is describing an occurrence that is frequent in everyday life. We often observe that an experience that we had eagerly anticipated is not at all satisfying, while an experience that we had dreaded is not upsetting. Simon maintains that the reason for such occurrences is that the "mind cannot at a single moment grasp the consequences in their entirety."[34] This does not appear to be so much an explanation of the phenomenon as another way of stating the problem. However, whether or not the reasons for the difficulty of anticipating value consequences accurately can be stated, the gap between anticipation and satisfaction is familiar to the great majority of human beings. Finally, complete rationality requires that the decider be aware of all the possible alternatives for action that he might choose. The common experience of realizing too late that one could have acted in a more efficient way is enough to show the restrictions on recognition of alternatives that most people confront. If we frequently realize that we have failed to take a possibility into account, how much more often do we remain completely unaware of alternatives?

In the face of incomplete information, difficulties of anticipation and restrictions on possibilities, human beings rely upon organizations to structure their decisions. Simon defines an organization as a pattern of communications and other relations in a group of human beings that provides to each member of the group "much of the information, assumptions, goals, and attitudes that enter into his decisions," as well as a "set of stable and comprehensible expectations as to what the other members of the group are doing and how they will react to what he says and does."[35] In brief, an organization places limits on the values that human beings seek to realize, the actions that they perform and the knowledge that they use to evaluate alternatives among permissible actions oriented toward the attainment of approved goals.

Organizations are characterized by what Simon calls vertical specialization and horizontal specialization. Horizontal specialization refers to what is often

---

[34] Simon, *Administrative Behavior*, p. 83.
[35] Simon, *Administrative Behavior*, p. xvi.

called division of labor. It is a way of dividing complex tasks into their component parts and assigning different human beings to perform the various actions necessary to fulfilling the task. For one person to construct an automobile from the raw materials that compose it would be an impossible task. A great many automobiles can be produced rapidly by a number of human beings performing specialized functions. A political example of horizontal specialization is the common division of the work of modern legislatures into subject area committees. While no legislator can be an expert in all of the major policy areas covered by contemporary law, a legislator can become an expert in one or two areas. The division of most of contemporary legislative work into specialized committees insures that some expertise is brought to bear in deliberations on laws. Vertical specialization is less familiar than horizontal specialization. It refers to specialization in decision making. Simon notes that wherever horizontal specialization is present, vertical specialization is a necessity to attain coordination. Someone must have the authority to decide, at different levels of the organization, how resources are allocated. Vertical specialization occurs even in legislatures. Legislative leaders decide which bills are given priority and how much time is allotted to their consideration. Thus, they have authority. For Simon authority is defined as the "power to make decisions which guide the actions of another."[36] Thus, one has authority over another person when his decisions become premises of the decisions of the other. Every organization has an authority structure, although that structure may not be best conceived of as a pyramid. The president of the United States may take as premises of many of his decisions the suggestions of the Secret Service agents assigned to protect him. With respect to the kind of automobile he travels in or the route that he takes from a hotel to an airport, he may follow the advice of his agents without question. With regard to these matters he allows the agents to exercise authority over him, to determine the premises of his decisions. Simon stresses that in any complex organization the authority structure can be most adequately conceived of as a complicated web.

The choices of individuals who participate in organizations are restricted by both horizontal specialization and vertical specialization. Horizontal specialization restricts the knowledge and the skills that individuals can bring to bear on the performance of tasks. Vertical specialization restricts the power of individuals to determine the premises of the decisions of others. Those with the most authority in an organization have the most influence in determining the goals that will be sought by participants in the organization.

However, Simon argues that the goals of an organization are always the result of a compromise among various groups. Here Simon develops his analysis in a way similar to Truman's discussion. Since the objectives of an

---

[36] Simon, *Administrative Behavior*, p. 125.

organization are unlikely to accord completely with any particular individual's preferences, organizations must offer inducements for participation. Simon identifies three bases for participation in organizations. One may participate in an organization because he derives, or expects to derive, personal rewards from the accomplishment of the organization's goals. One may participate in an organization because he derives, or expects to derive, personal rewards from the size and growth of the organization. Finally, one may participate in an organization because he derives, or expects to derive, personal rewards offered by the organization but unrelated to its size and growth. The three reasons for participation correspond to three kinds of participants: customers, entrepreneurs and employees. In return for benefits participants make contributions to the organization: customers contribute money or services, entrepreneurs contribute the materials on which work is done, and employees contribute time and effort. Organizations continue to function as long as they are able to elicit contributions that are at least equivalent to the inducements for participation that they must offer.

The ultimate answer to the question—How are choices contained in organizations?—is that the values or goals sought by organizations restrict decisions. Simon remarks that the fundamental standards of value that will be used in making decisions among alternatives in an organization "will be selected for the organization primarily by the controlling group—the group that has the power to set the terms of membership for all the participants."[37] The group that can determine the basic standards of value will try to attain its particular values through the organization. However, this group, as far as it exists, is limited in the control that it can exert by the need to offer inducements for the contributions of other participants. This is the reason why the objectives sought in any complex organization represent a compromise among the goals of various groups. Of course, this does not mean that some groups may not be far more influential in determining the premises of the decisions of participants than others. It means that whatever the personal values of controlling groups happen to be, they will have to be partly motivated by the objective of merely maintaining the structure of the organization. Simon is far less impressed by the limiting power of internalized norms than most of the other current theorists whom we have discussed. While he argues that decisions in organizations are restricted by value premises, he believes that in great part these value premises represent the preferences of groups that control the organizations.

Imaginative Perspective

To adopt the perspective of Simon's decision-making theory is to clarify the world of common sense. It is easy to recognize "administrative man" any-

---

[37] Simon, *Administrative Behavior*, p. 118.

where in the contemporary world. In most organizational relationships and situations people are confronted with the problems of defining their goals, gathering information about how to best realize their projects and attempting to predict how other people will behave. Most people do not have perfectly consistent scales of preference and they are not sure how the objectives of the organizations in which they participate accord with their own goals. Further, everyone acts in the face of incomplete information about the possible ways in which to realize their goals and the future behaviors of significant others. Within the boundaries set by the human situation, horizontal specialization and vertical specialization, many people satisfice. From the personal point of view they attempt to get as many personal rewards from the organizations as they can. If they are administrators they attempt to get as many resources for their agencies as they can. As a result of the structure of inducements they may identify with the objectives of their organizations, the sheer growth and maintenance of their organizations, or both.

The experience of satisficing is not romantic and neither is the prospect of identifying one's own goals with the goals of an organization. Simon would probably reply to critics of his vision by maintaining that human beings are capable of no more than satisficing and that if the goals of organizations are comprehensive and generous they can be worthy of one's commitment. There is nothing intrinsically dull about Simon's vision. Antipathy toward complex organizations may be less a result of organizational life in general than of the content of contemporary organizational goals.

Peter M. Blau

Peter M. Blau is a sociological theorist who has devoted much of his attention to the dynamics of organizational relations and the questions of political theory.* His first book, *The Dynamics of Bureaucracy,* represented an attempt to demonstrate the thesis that "bureaucratic structures continually create conditions that modify these structures."[38] He developed his analysis of the social relations present in a public employment agency and a law enforcement agency under the basic tenet that the "social consequences of phenomena, not merely their origins, must be taken into account in socio-logical inquiry."[39] By a study of the social consequences of phenomena, Blau meant that organization theorists should attempt to account for the effects of specific relations and practices upon the adjustment or functioning of organ-

---

*Many of the ideas in this section are drawn from Michael A. Weinstein and Deena Weinstein, "Blau's Dialectical Sociology," a paper presented at the meetings of the Southern Sociological Society, April, 1970.

[38] Peter M. Blau, *The Dynamics of Bureaucracy* (Chicago: University of Chicago Press, 1963), p. 8.

[39] Blau, *The Dynamics,* p. 7.

izations. Like the systems theorists and group theorists whom we have already discussed, Blau was concerned with the contributions that various social relations made to the maintenance of a social structure. However, instead of making the entire political or social system his basic unit of analysis, he viewed activities and relations from the point of view of the organization. Since the publication of *The Dynamics of Bureaucracy* Blau has written several other books about the theory of social organization. In *Bureaucracy in Modern Society* he reviewed the literature of complex organizations.[40] In *Formal Organizations* Blau and W. Richard Scott developed a theory of organizations that departed from the standpoint of systems theory and its concern with the problem of order.[41] Thus far, Blau's major work has been *Exchange and Power in Social Life,* in which he presents a "dialectical" view of social relations within organizations.[42] In our discussion of Blau's organization theory we will be primarily concerned with the questions posed and the concepts developed in *Formal Organizations* and *Exchange and Power in Social Life.*

The Political Questions

The questions raised by Blau fall within two families of queries. In *Formal Organizations* he works within the tradition of political theory that responds to the question: Who gets what, when and how? Specifically, Blau and Scott ask, *Cui bono?*—Who benefits? They develop a classification of organizations by defining the characteristic groups that benefit from organizations. Blau and Scott identify four types of contemporary organizations that correspond to four groups of prime beneficiaries. Mutual benefit associations, like labor unions and even democratic governments, have the membership as their prime beneficiaries. Business concerns have the owners as their prime beneficiaries; service organizations, like universities and hospitals, have their clients as the prime beneficiaries; and commonweal organizations, like police forces and armies, have the public-at-large as their prime beneficiaries. For Blau and Scott, each type of organization confronts a characteristic structural dilemma that is related to its function of serving a particular group, or prime beneficiary. Mutual benefit associations face the problem of maintaining democratic control by the membership while at the same time acting decisively in the interest of the membership. Truman noted this problem in his discussion of the structure of interest groups, and it is well to note that

---

[40] Peter M. Blau, *Bureaucracy in Modern Society* (New York: Random House, 1956).
[41] Peter M. Blau and W. Richard Scott, *Formal Organizations* (San Francisco: Chandler Press, 1962).
[42] Peter M. Blau, *Exchange and Power in Social Life* (New York: John Wiley and Sons, 1967).

mutual benefit associations that make demands on other social groups for allocations of resources or actions are political interest groups.

Business concerns encounter the problem of maximizing efficiency under the strains of competition. The difficulties of attaining efficiency were discussed by Simon in his analysis of the limits of rationality in organizations. Complete information about alternatives, clarity about organizational goals, knowledge of the means to attaining goals and loyalty of members to the organization would all tend to increase efficiency. The less these ideals are approached, the less efficiency is possible. Efficiency is always relative, a matter of degree.

Service organizations confront the problem of attaining maximum professional service to clients while maintaining regularized administration. An example of this kind of conflict is the student-teacher relationship in universities. Perhaps the ideal way to learn and teach political theory would be for students and teachers to meet when reading, conversations or events raised general questions. When people were ready to enter dialogue or discussion they would continue as long as necessary. However, the ideal method of political education developed by Socrates is not applied in contemporary universities. Requirements for degrees must be set, classroom space scheduled at certain hours and course content standardized. In this case administrative requirements restrict professional service. This does not mean that administration should be eliminated. Given limited resources and an insistent demand for higher education, the ideal of individualized instruction and discussion in small groups is sacrificed to the goal of a university education for more people. To approach the ideal while retaining mass higher education would require more resources allocated to university teaching.

Commonweal organizations encounter the problem of attaining maximum democratic control of their operations while efficiently performing their specialized services. The demands for civilian review boards of police activities and the counter-demands that the police be permitted to perform their functions with minimum public control illustrate this dilemma.

Blau and Scott distinguish their approach from Simon's mode of analysis. While Simon argues that the function of the organization is to "limit the scope of the decisions that each member must make" by defining the responsibility of each official ("thus supplying him with goals to guide his decisions") and by setting up formal rules, information channels and programs (thus narrowing the "range of alternatives the official must consider before making his decisions"), Blau and Scott maintain that organizations function to benefit different groups.[43] They hold that the importance of the *cui bono* criterion for defining the character of organizations is "indicated by

---

[43] Blau and Scott, *Formal Organizations*, p. 37.

the fundamental changes that occur when there is a shift in the prime
beneficiary from one to another of the four categories."[44] They note that
such changes in the prime beneficiary are frequently accompanied by intense
social conflict and are often termed "revolutionary." Perhaps Simon, and Blau
and Scott are not completely opposed in their thinking. Simon distinguishes
among customers, entrepreneurs and employees, as participants in organizations, and holds that the group that has the most power in an organization
has the most decisive influence on the goals that the organization will pursue.
Blau and Scott also identify groups of organizational participants and argue
that the dynamics of organizational behavior can be explained, in great part,
by naming the prime beneficiaries of particular organizations. In fact, Simon's
types of participants and the prime beneficiaries of Blau and Scott are
interchangeable. The prime beneficiaries of service organizations and commonweal organizations are customers (clients and the public-at-large); the
prime beneficiaries of business concerns are entrepreneurs (owners), and the
prime beneficiaries of mutual benefit associations are employees (membership). At least there is the hint of a linkage here between theories that
respond to the question, Who gets what, when and how? (Who benefits?); and
theories that respond to the question, How do systems persist? (How are
choices restricted in organizations?)

In *Exchange and Power in Social Life* Blau returns to the kind of question
that occupies systems theorists. He states that the "basic question that is
being raised is how social life becomes organized into increasingly complex
structures of associations among men."[45] Out of all of the possible relations
among human beings Blau attempts to "derive the social processes that
govern the complex structures of communities and societies from the simpler
processes that pervade the daily intercourse among individuals and their
interpersonal relations."[46] Blau's concentration on the problem of how
relations between human beings become organized into complex structures
places him in the same universe of discourse as Simon.

The Fundamental Concepts

While Simon discusses administrative behavior in terms of concepts that are
rooted in economics and modified for the purposes of organization theory, he
primarily attends to the problems of the individual decision maker within the
organization. Blau, who in *Exchange and Power in Social Life* also uses
concepts that originate in economics, concerns himself with relations among
human beings. For Blau, the basic processes that determine associations

---

[44] Blau and Scott, *Formal Organizations*, p. 44.
[45] Blau, *Exchange and Power*, p. 2.
[46] Blau, *Exchange and Power*, p. 2.

among human beings may be described under the terms exchange or reciprocity. When one human being furnishes assistance to another he comes under an obligation to reciprocate. This does not mean that payment for aid must be in money or kind. Sometimes expressions of gratitude are enough to exchange for something desired. However, while a person may be willing to accept gratitude a few times, "he can hardly be expected regularly to devote time and effort to providing help without receiving any return to compensate him for his troubles."[47] A person who needs aid from an associate, but who has nothing but gratitude to exchange for it, can take several courses of action. He can force the associate to help him, obtain help from another source, find ways to get along without help or "subordinate himself to the other and comply with his wishes."[48] In the last situation the person allows his associate to determine some of the premises of his decisions. He submits himself to the authority of the associate in some contexts of activity, or, as Blau puts it, he rewards the associate with power over himself as "an inducement for furnishing the needed help."[49] Thus, Blau defines the basic "dialectic" or opposition present in social relations. Out of the situation of reciprocity, or equal exchange, the relation of power, or fundamental inequality develops. The content of *Exchange and Power in Social Life* is a development and elaboration of the interplay between the two concepts.

Perhaps the most important application of the concepts "exchange" and "power" for political theory is Blau's discussion of authority. Blau distinguishes among power and authority. Power relationships are characterized by an individual allowing another person to determine some of the premises of his decisions. Authority arises out of formally organized power relationships. A manager or an official is often in a position to contribute to the welfare of a group of subordinates. Such contributions create an obligation on the group members to repay the official in some way. These joint obligations "tend to find expression in group norms that demand compliance" with the official's directives.[50] When such group norms are operative new members of the group will be taught to obey directives not by the official, but by the other members of the group. Members of the group who refuse to obey directives will be disciplined by the rest of the group. Thus, the official will be able to gain voluntary compliance with his demands "independent of any enforcement action on his part." For Blau, authority grows out of exchange and power. The official initially has power. In exchange for favors that he does for a group of subordinates, the group takes over some of the enforcement of compliance with the official's directives. In

---

[47] Blau, *Exchange and Power*, p. 21.
[48] Blau, *Exchange and Power*, p. 21.
[49] Blau, *Exchange and Power*, p. 22.
[50] Blau, *Exchange and Power*, p. 222.

a situation characterized by authority, the premises of the subordinate's decision are determined vertically and laterally. The premises of officials are adopted in part *because* one's peers insist that they become decisional premises. The stresses on political nonconformists are partly due to the persistence of authority relationships in the political system.

Neither the basic processes of exchange and power, nor the emergence of authority relationships can account for how "social life becomes organized into increasingly complex structures of associations among men."[51] After developing the concepts of exchange, power and authority, Blau answers his fundamental question in the traditional terms of systems theory. He states that commonly "accepted social values serve as media of social transactions that extend the range of social processes beyond the limits of direct social contacts through large collectivities and long periods of time."[52] Complex structures of associations, such as organizations, governments and interest groups, will persist if values become regularized in formal procedures, are transmitted to the young and are supported by powerful groups. For Blau, as for Easton and Truman, shared values and norms make the persistence of organizations possible.

Imaginative Perspective

Blau's political world is one in which the tensions of ordinary living are experienced with a clarity absent in everyday life. Human beings are enmeshed in a complex web of relations that they cannot escape. In order to gain what one wants, one must seek the aid of others. In return for help one must give something of value to the associate in exchange. The individual is fortunate if he need only surrender money to gain some satisfaction of his desires. Most people have to surrender some of their autonomy in return for goods, services and even sociable relations. They have to restrict their decisions by adopting the premises of others. Further, they are caught within peer groups that enforce obedience to superiors in position. From a view of social life that began with the processes of sociability, reciprocity and free exchange, an almost nightmarish vision of control emerges. Of course, the suffocation of the individual is minimized to the extent that he accepts the social values that prevail in his groups. However, more than any of the other writers we have considered, Blau shows the barriers in the way of attaining autonomy. When we aid others over a period of time, we normally expect to be repaid in some way. We are painfully aware that others have the same

---

[51] Blau, *Exchange and Power*, p. 222.
[52] Blau, *Exchange and Power*, p. 280.

expectations when they aid us. It is from such elementary considerations that Blau believes our social lives arise.

Heinz Eulau

Heinz Eulau has been at the forefront of research on legislative behavior, particularly the analysis of representational processes. Like many current political theorists, he has worked in two eras of the history of political science. At the beginning of his career he was close to political events and served as assistant editor of the liberal opinion journal *New Republic*. When, in the 1950s, the intellectual revolution that ushered in the behavioral approach to the study of politics gathered force, Eulau became one of its leaders. Trained in traditional literary, historical and legal methods of analyzing political and governmental phenomena, Eulau underwent the rigors of learning the statistical and questionnaire methods required by the behavioral approach. The great discipline, effort and adaptability required by such a reorientation of intellectual life is evidence of the energy and commitment that the leaders of the behavioral movement were able to marshal. If some of the optimism that accompanied programs for a scientific study of politics is now gone, it is well to remember that the early behavioralists felt that they had embarked on an exciting adventure. The behavioralists attempted to penetrate every zone of political life to learn how political actors really behaved and, in Eulau's terms, what political activity meant to participants. Eulau chose legislative behavior as his specialty and with John Wahlke, William Buchanan and LeRoy C. Ferguson contributed to and brought together a set of studies on legislatures and representation, *The Legislative System*.[53] In 1963 Eulau published *The Behavioral Persuasion in Politics*, an essay defining his mature thoughts on the meaning of the behavioral revolution for the conduct of political science.[54] While he adopted the essay form to convey his ideas and thereby sacrificed systematic exposition for ease in accessibility, *The Behavioral Persuasion in Politics* contains a theory of political life that is rooted in the study of political subsystems. Perhaps Eulau would identify the framework of ideas that he presents as an approach rather than a theory because he mainly defines concepts rather than developing explanatory statements. However, like the other current political theorists, he poses a basic question, defines fundamental concepts in response to that question and presents an imaginative perspective on political life. In our

---

[53] John C. Wahlke, *et al., The Legislative System: Explorations in Legislative Behavior* (New York: John Wiley and Sons, 1962).

[54] Heinz Eulau, *The Behavioral Persuasion in Politics* (New York: Random House, 1963).

discussion of Eulau's ideas we will rely primarily on the analysis that appears in *The Behavioral Persuasion in Politics.*

The Political Question

Like Truman, Simon and Blau, Eulau clearly states the question around which he organizes his political studies. He says that the "simple question" he wants to ask is, "Why do people behave politically as they do?"[55] Unlike the other questions that we have considered, Eulau's query does not seem to imply the problem of order (How do political systems persist under stress?) or what we will later call the problem of power (Who gets what, when and how? *Cui bono?*). Instead, the query directs us to attempt to describe the conditions under which various political activities occur. Of course, behind Eulau's simple question is a wide area of ambiguity and vagueness.

As in the case of Truman's analysis, where the term "polity" was ill-defined, Eulau's discussion is hampered by a lack of clarity about the use of the term "political." Unless we are told what it means to "behave politically" we will not be able to describe the conditions in which people undertake political behavior. Eulau registers an objection to the contention that he should define the term "political." He argues that the study of politics and government in the past has been greatly impeded by what he calls immanent or essentialist definitions of politics. An immanent or essentialist definition states the conditions under which a phenomenon will be given a certain name. For example, if politics is defined as the authoritative allocation of values for a society, only those phenomena that are related to the process of authoritatively allocating values for a society will be characterized by the adjective "political." Eulau points out that the traditional way of starting an investigation of anything was to define the subject matter under analysis and draw boundaries. This style of analysis, of course, led to endless squabbles in every field of knowledge about the "essence" of the particular subject matter. Thus, political theorists might argue about whether politics was the art of ordering society for the attainment of the common good, the art of attaining power or highway robbery. Like other behavioral theorists, Eulau deplores polemics over definitions and desires to get on with the study of behavior. However, he cannot avoid the task of setting some boundaries to his discussion. While Eulau repeats such statements as the study of political behavior is concerned with the acts of human beings in "political contexts," eventually he defines politics in a way that his question becomes meaningful in relation to the queries of the other current political theorists we have considered.

Eulau states that, at least in part, politics is "purposive activity through which a group—whether a national society at one end of the matrix or the

---

[55] Eulau, *The Behavioral Persuasion,* p. 3..

nuclear family at the other end—engages in collective decision-making."[56] Further, he contends that a definition of politics as the authoritative alloca- tion of values for a society is not broad enough unless it is supplemented by the idea that political behavior is related to interhuman conflict. From a consideration of this definition Eulau's basic political question can be re- phrased and compared to the questions posed by the other current political theorists. Eulau's query is, Why do people engage in some forms of collective decision making rather than others? This query seems to be most like the questions posed by Deutsch and Simon. For Deutsch, governance is a process of steering collective efforts toward goals. For Simon, politics is a process through which collective choices are limited. In all three cases the primary concern is with how order is brought out of chaos. In a sense, all of the political theories that take the problem of order as their basis are political extensions of the Second Law of Thermodynamics which states that closed systems tend toward a state of entropy, or a state of uniform distribution of energy. Chaos is the normal state of affairs, while order requires effort, or a concentration of energy. Eulau is in the tradition of political theorists who pose the problem of order. Of course, Eulau differs from some of the systems theorists. For example, he holds that political behavior occurs wherever there are processes of collective decision making. Easton, on the other hand, is concerned with the processes of collective decision making for entire societies. A similar contrast could be made between Eulau and Truman. An examination of Eulau's fundamental concepts will show just how much his work has been influenced by the problem of order.

The Fundamental Concepts

Eulau's fundamental concepts are organized to answer the question, Why do people engage in some forms of collective decision making rather than others? As a first response to this query he remarks that behavior always precedes formal structure. In other words, the process of ruling should be analyzed before the structure of government, the process of obeying before the structure of authority, the process of representing before the structure of legislatures. In discussing how these processes are best described, Eulau defines his central concept of role. From a "social matrix" characterized by "interactions and transactions that orient people towards each other, making them mutually responsive," standardized expectations of behavior in particu- lar contexts arise.[57] Eulau calls these standardized expectations of behavior "roles," and he remarks that a "person is identified by his role and that, in interpersonal relations activating the role, he behaves, will behave, or should behave in certain ways."[58] For Eulau role is a concept that unites all of the

[56] Eulau, *The Behavioral Persuasion*, p. 59.
[57] Eulau, *The Behavioral Persuasion*, p. 39.
[58] Eulau, *The Behavioral Persuasion*, p. 40.

levels of analysis of human behavior. Eulau identifies three levels of analysis in the human sciences. On the cultural level of analysis human products, both mental and physical, are investigated. With respect to role analysis, cultural investigation requires that the student describe the norms, expectations, rights and duties that characterize human relationships. On the social level of analysis, meaningful interactions between human beings are investigated. With respect to role analysis, social investigation requires that the student describe actual interactions and compare their course to what is culturally expected. On the personal level of analysis, the personalities of individual human beings are investigated. With respect to role analysis, investigation of the political personality requires that the unique role definitions held by different people be described. On each level of analysis political roles are being studied. In other words, the role theorist describes patterns of expectation, behavior and choice that are related to the processes of collective decision making.

Roles emerge from human interactions. Therefore, every interaction that is culturally defined has one or more roles associated with it. In some cases relations are characterized by unipolar roles such as leader-follower, representative-constituent, prosecutor-defense attorney. Each role in a set of unipolar roles implies the other. Often a person is associated with a set of roles that are closely connected with one another. A change in one role will likely force changes in the closely related roles. Eulau calls such a cluster of roles a "role system." Role systems may be characterized by a vaguely defined role that provides a name for a generalized activity. Such a vague role, in which the expected behaviors are not clear, is the role of politician.

Roles are no more than the cross sections of activity that formed the basis of the political theories of Easton and Truman. Easton held that the cross sections of activity had meaning in terms of a system oriented toward the process of authoritatively allocating values for a society. Truman held that the cross sections of activity had meaning in terms of interests in the continuation and expansion of human activities. For Eulau, the cross sections of activity have meaning for collective decision making because they bring order out of chaos. He observes that if a "relationship had to be defined anew with each interaction, or if expectations had to be elaborated with every new encounter, stable social life would be impossible."[59] Stable social life, or predictable patterns of collective decision making, are made possible by a "broad cultural consensus as to what the rights and duties pertaining to social roles are, and there is consensus on the sanctions available to participants in a relationship if behavior should violate agreed-on norms."[60] Thus, Eulau responds to the problem of order in the same way as the other current political theorists who consider this problem. Political systems persist through

---

[59] Eulau, *The Behavioral Persuasion,* p. 43.
[60] Eulau, *The Behavioral Persuasion,* p. 43.

change, patterns of collective decision making persist because people by and large conform to culturally defined standards of appropriate political behavior. The major difference between Eulau and the other theorists is that while they described the entire political system, or groups and organizations within it, he describes the roles that make up these systems and subsystems.

In his description of role theory, Eulau does not imply that political life is devoid of serious conflict. Eulau distinguishes between homogeneous groups which take their patterns of role behavior for granted and heterogeneous groups which "are forever in search of meanings that give their behavior symbolic significance."[61] Where significant complexities in social structure exist conflicts between ideal role patterns and "operative ideals" are likely to appear. Such conflicts between cultural ideals and the goals actually sought in social relationships are a central source of political tensions. In a profound sense, political conflict is conflict over the definition of roles. Eulau remarks that "political institutions are cultural products par excellance," because "by definition, an institution is a set of widely shared, regularized patterns of behavior that are fairly stable through time."[62] When groups in a society challenge existing institutions they are actually challenging role systems. They seek either to bring operative conceptions of rights and duties into line with ideal role patterns, or they attempt to introduce new role definitions into the culture. The construct of a particular political culture is a "summary expression" of a large number of individual patterns of behavior, and it is subject to continuous change as disputes about role definitions arise and are decided. Contemporary societies resemble heterogeneous groups, forever in search of meanings that give their behavior symbolic significance. Within them people by and large conform to culturally defined standards of appropriate political behavior, but these standards provide for a minimal rather than a maximal order in public affairs and circumscribe important conflicts.

Imaginative Perspective

Eulau states that the root and the goal of political science, particularly in its behavioral aspect, should be man. He is concerned, however, about what image of the human being a behavioral theorist can hold. He asks, "Which is the man in whose service the behavioral persuasion finds its reason for existence?"[63] After listing some of the traditional immanent and essentialist definitions of the human being such as the human as power-seeker, depraved sinner and creator, Eulau concludes that the "most we can say is that different men have different conceptions of man and, as a result, give different meanings to what they do and why they do it."[64] Thus, just

---

[61] Eulau, *The Behavioral Persuasion*, p. 70.
[62] Eulau, *The Behavioral Persuasion*, pp. 68-69.
[63] Eulau, *The Behavioral Persuasion*, p. 133.
[64] Eulau, *The Behavioral Persuasion*, pp. 133-34.

as Eulau attempted to discuss politics without defining its essence, he also attempts to leave the human being without an essence. One makes oneself. One can be defined by no one, not even by the behavioral scientist. There are always conflicts between and within roles, and roles are always vague at the penumbra. Choice is a necessity. Perhaps, just as Eulau eventually gave a definition of politics appropriate to the question that he posed, there are also contextual definitions of the human being that arise from the questions that people ask about themselves. Whether or not there are definitions of the human being implied in our discussions of the human plight, Eulau's role theory demonstrates how the behavioral approach can connect with the existentialist's doctrine that human existence precedes human essence. In Eulau's terms, behavior precedes structure.

Theories
of
Political
Influence

4

While theories of the political system and political subsystems represented attempts to penetrate beyond the surface conflicts of everyday political life to the factors that limit and pattern these conflicts, theories of political influence are more oriented toward the investigation of everyday political life. The question posed by theorists of the political system and political subsystems—How do political systems persist through stressful change?—is not obvious and is derived from successive developments in the history of Western political thought since the time of Thomas Hobbes. The problem of order is not a question that bothers the practical politician. The idea of a political system and the notion of cross sections of human activity on which it is based are abstractions not frequently found in everyday experience. They are conceptions developed for the scientific observer of political life rather than for the citizen or the politician. The questions posed by theorists of political influence—Who gets what, when and how? and, Who governs?—have preoccupied thoughtful people at least since the time of Plato. In any society in which social relationships are more extensive than face-to-face contacts some people speculate about who makes the significant decisions that pattern social life. In the history of political thought there have been two general responses to the question, Who governs? Theorists of political elites have argued that in any society significant decisions are made by a relatively small group of people who share certain common interests and styles of life. Theorists of political pluralism have argued that in at least some societies significant decisions are made by many different individuals and groups who do not share sets of well-defined common interests and may differ sharply in their styles of life. Theorists of political systems and political subsystems have usually not directly entered the debate between theorists of political elites and theorists of political pluralism. Theorists like David Easton and Herbert Simon are apt to argue that authoritative allocations of values and decisional premises are so significantly shaped by cultural norms and values that the problem of who rules is relatively unimportant in the explanation of political affairs. For theorists of the political system and political subsystems the norms and values really govern. Of course, some theorists who ask the question—How do political systems persist through stressful change?—investigate the problem of the distribution of influence. David Truman and other interest group theorists have taken the side of the pluralists when discussing the distribution of influence in the United States.

Theorists of political elites and theorists of political pluralism have challenged the emphasis that systems theorists place on cultural norms and values in explaining political affairs. They point out that the norms and values of any particular culture are not neutral in their consequences for different social groups. For example, norms favoring the protection of private property work more to the benefit of owners than in the interest of propertyless individuals. The most fervent theorists of political influence maintain that the norms and values that characterize a particular culture are merely devices that perpetuate the power of governing elites. They argue that these norms and values are embodied in symbols that the members of ruling groups manipulate to gain favorable responses from the ruled. Theorists of political elites like Gaetano Mosca have held that each ruling class develops a "political formula" to justify its power to the ruled and thereby gain the acquiescence of the ruled with a minimum expenditure of resources. It is doubtful that theorists of political systems and political subsystems are correct in placing so much emphasis on the significance of cultural norms and values for the patterning of political behavior. It is equally unlikely that theorists of political influence are correct in placing so much emphasis on the significance of power structures for explaining political affairs. The two positions are probably complementary and perhaps imply one another. On the simplest level of analysis, it is clear that norms and values are supported by power structures at the same time they limit the uses to which power is put. Current political theorists are far from appreciating the subtle relationships between conflict and consensus, interest and norm, even though they have cleared the way for such investigations by providing responses to their basic questions. Particularly in the dialectical conceptions of Peter Blau, which we have discussed under the heading of theories of political subsystems, there is promise of modes of analysis that can aid in the discovery of relationships between seemingly opposed terms.

The Political Questions

The questions—Who governs? and, Who gets what, when and how?—appear to be appeals for descriptions rather than explanations. The same observation holds true for the basic question posed by theorists of the political system and political subsystems, How do political systems persist through stressful change? In neither case does the theorist seem to be asking why certain events occur, or under what conditions certain events take place. However, it would be a mistake to assume that either theorists of political systems and political subsystems, or theorists of political influence are more interested in descriptions than explanations. Behind the questions of "who" and "how" are queries concerning why certain persons and groups have come to govern and why certain political systems persist. This point is important to keep in mind because current political theorists are often accused of evading the scientific task of seeking explanations for the occurrence of political events. This criticism is frequently the result of a superficial analysis of the basic questions posed by current political theorists and the concepts that they develop in response to these queries. While most current political theorists do not provide research designs through which their major explanatory hypotheses can be tested, they do offer such hypotheses. Thus, the questions—Who governs? and, Who gets what, when and how?—are far more complex than they first appear. The theorists who pose them would not be satisfied if one could point to a group of people and say, "They rule around here." Theorists of political influence are concerned with clarifying exactly what it means to make a decision and to exercise influence, analyzing how decisions are made in actual political systems and, particularly, investigating why some individuals and groups gain more influence than others.

Theorists of political influence have been responding to the question of who governs for several thousand years. Among the Greek political thinkers, both Plato and Aristotle devised sophisticated classification systems for identifying possible ruling groups. Plato distinguished among political systems controlled by elites of wisdom, military power, wealth, popularity and naked brutality. He ranked these regimes in a descending order of moral excellence. Aristotle distinguished among political systems controlled by one ruler, a small group of leaders and a large portion of the population. He further divided all political systems into those in which rule was exercised in the public interest and those in which rule was exercised in the interest of the governing group only. In current political theories of the behavioral persuasion the moral emphasis of the Greek political thinkers is lacking. However, the basic descriptive categories of the Greeks, particularly Plato, are still fundamental in theories of political influence. In Plato's scheme of categorizing political systems, there are emphases on the political formulae that elites employ to legitimize their rule, the kinds of life styles that characterize the different elites, the types of personalities that gain influence in various regimes and the different bases for elite power. These four emphases are present in current theories of political influence. Harold Lasswell, a theorist of political elites, has developed a list of political values that different political elites seek to monopolize. This list resembles Plato's categorization of political values into wisdom, courage, wealth, popularity and power. Robert Dahl, a theorist of political pluralism, has investigated the problems of the bases of political power and the life styles of people who engage in American politics. His discussion of the differences between civic man and political man finds a parallel in Aristotle's discussion of the citizen. Both Lasswell and Dahl are concerned with the political formulae that leaders employ to justify their rule and gain support. Lasswell analyzes symbol manipulation as a technique of elite domination and Dahl discusses the "rituals" of American democracy.

Influence as a Key Political Concept

While influence or power have long been regarded as fundamental political concepts there is still much vagueness involved in their use. Both Lasswell and Dahl prefer to use influence as their key political concept. Their differing analyses of the term point up some of its ambiguities and difficulties. For Lasswell, the "study of politics is the study of influence and the influential."[1] He has a very clear-cut and simple definition of influence: "The influential are those who get the most of what there is to get. . . . Those who get the most are *elite;* the rest are *mass.*"[2] Thus, Lasswell defines influence as the acquisition of socially available values. People exercise influence in their attempts to acquire and protect socially available values. Lasswell identifies four important methods through which influence is exercised in politics. Individuals and groups may manipulate symbols, apply violence, give and withhold economic goods and modify decision-making procedures to acquire socially available values. The best index of influence is the distribution of socially available values.

For Dahl, the problem of influence is much more complex than it is for Lasswell. Dahl does not identify the distribution of socially available values with the distribution of influence. He notes that socially available values may be used as resources for influencing decisions. However, he is careful to

---

[1] Harold D. Lasswell, *Politics: Who Gets What, When, How* (Cleveland: The World Publishing Company, 1958), p. 13.

[2] Lasswell, *Politics,* p. 13.

distinguish between the possession of resources and their actual use in the decision-making process. Dahl would claim that one may be extremely wealthy and have no appreciable political influence. A wealthy person who did not use his resources to finance political campaigns, influence public opinion or lobby in legislatures or administrative agencies would probably have little direct influence over particular decisions. Dahl states that influence can be defined as the probability that one will have his way on a particular decision, even if he meets opposition. He distinguishes between direct and indirect influence. One has direct influence when he actually contributes to the decision-making process. One has indirect influence when those directly involved in the decision-making process take his presumed preferences into account when they are choosing. Once the distinction between direct and indirect influence is made it becomes evident that the concept of influence is difficult. Some of these difficulties can be exposed by referring back to the example of the wealthy individual who does not devote his resources to political activities. While Dahl is correct, by definition, that this person has little or no direct political influence, he may have a great deal of indirect political influence. He may not have to engage in political activities because politicians are careful not to offend him, lest he use his resources to displace them. Alternatively, he may not have to engage in political activities because politicians already share his policy preferences. In this case, the politicians may not even be aware that they are faithfully representing the wealthy individual. Finally, he may not have to engage in political activities because no decisions of consequence to him are made in the political system. This last alternative is quite unlikely in contemporary industrialized societies. The difficulties of the concept of indirect influence make it nearly impossible to measure the impact that various individuals and groups have on the decision-making process in a complex industrialized society like the United States. However, it is hard to disagree with Dahl that there is a difference between the acquisition of socially available values and the actual use of these resources to influence political decisions. Perhaps the distribution of socially available values provides a rough index of the distribution of indirect influence in a society. Certainly, to investigate direct influence one would have to study the decisions that are made on various issues, as Dahl has done.

A theorist who takes seriously the role of indirect influence in political decisions is likely to be a theorist of political elites. A theorist who concentrates more on the role of direct influence in political decisions is likely to be a theorist of political pluralism. It will be useful to keep this distinction in mind when following the succeeding discussion of the political theories of Harold Lasswell and Robert Dahl.

Harold Lasswell

Harold Lasswell was among the first American political theorists to adopt the program of advancing a scientific study of politics. As early as the 1920s Lasswell was working on the possible applications in political theory of the concepts developed in depth psychiatry and personality theory. Lasswell's thought was finally embodied in *Psychopathology and Politics*, which he published in 1930.[3] In this volume Lasswell argued that much of political behavior could be explained as a reflection of deep-seated emotional problems stemming from the individual's early childhood experiences. The appearance of *Psychopathology and Politics* was followed by *World Politics and Personal Insecurity* which was published in 1935.[4] In this book Lasswell extended the ideas developed in his earlier work to broader political contexts. In 1936 Lasswell published the theoretical essay, *Politics: Who Gets What, When, How,* which summarized his ideas about the form that a scientific political theory should take and the content that it should include.[5] Like Truman, another pioneer in behavioral political theory who was influenced by a group theory of politics developed at the beginning of the twentieth century, Lasswell drew upon the work of Gaetano Mosca, who propounded an elite theory of politics in the late nineteenth century.[6] The *Politics* included discussions of the relationships between personality and public acts, the processes of political communication and the characteristics of ruling classes and elites. These three themes have been of uppermost importance in Lasswell's later work. Since World War II Lasswell has continued to deepen his analyses of these topics. Typical of his continuing concern with the relationships between psychology and political science is the essay *Democratic Character,* published in 1951.[7] In this work Lasswell attempted to define the kind of personality type most likely to sustain democratic political institutions. Lasswell has also cooperated with the philosopher Abraham Kaplan in a study of power, written on the methods of studying elites and produced essays on the methods of studying communication, particularly propaganda. He has also studied the relationships between law and politics. Perhaps of all of the pioneers in behavioral political theory Lasswell has had the most influence on later theorizing and empirical research. Although a later generation of political theorists replaced Lasswell's basic political

---

[3]Harold D. Lasswell, *The Political Writings of Harold D. Lasswell* (Glencoe: The Free Press, 1951).
[4]Harold D. Lasswell, *World Politics and Personal Insecurity* (New York: Whittlesey House, 1935).
[5]Harold D. Lasswell, *Politics: Who Gets What, When, How.*
[6]Gaetano Mosca, *The Ruling Class* (New York: McGraw-Hill Book Company, 1939).
[7]Harold D. Lasswell, *The Political Writings of Harold D. Lasswell.*

question—Who gets what, when, and how?—with the query—Why do political systems persist under stress?—current political theorists still use many of Lasswell's fundamental concepts. Lasswell was interested in almost every theory and research area that is important in contemporary political science. He was even concerned with the recommendation of policies and schemes for attaining world peace and speeding social reconstruction. In *Psychopathology and Politics* he argued for a preventive politics that would require political leaders to undergo psychiatric examinations by a board of specialists before they could hold public office. In the *Politics* he proposed a mass movement that would cater to the interests of a new middle class whose members had sacrificed time and resources to attain socially useful skills. Lasswell believed that this group, which included employed people ranging in status from skilled worker to professional, would provide the members of the next governing elite in the West. Lasswell's stature as a political scientist whose writings and interests range across the subject matter and problems of the entire discipline has been equalled by no current political theorist. In our discussion of Lasswell's political theory we will concentrate on the ideas contained in the summary essay *Politics: Who Gets What, When, How.*

The Political Question

The theory of political activity contained in David Easton's *A Systems Analysis of Political Life* is particularly significant because it represents a self-conscious attempt to work out the implications of reorienting political studies from the problem of influence to the problem of order. Easton argued that the investigation of how political systems persist through change is more fundamental than the study of how political actors gain and retain influence. He contended that the question of who benefits from political activity implies that there is a context in which political activity is ordered. If it is correct that conflict over the distribution of values occurs in most societies, it is also true that the values sought are usually limited and definable, and that the methods used in prosecuting conflicts are normally restricted.

Lasswell might argue that just the opposite is true. Instead of asking how political systems persist through change, he queries, Who gets what, when, how? While he would certainly admit that in most societies a consensus on values and norms limits political activity, he would stress the importance of investigating the problem of why a consensus on some values and norms obtains rather than an agreement on others. This, he would argue, is a task closely bound up to that of discovering who is influential and who benefits from any given consensus. Perhaps the people who receive the highest values that a society has to offer are also the people who are most influential in determining the values that motivate and the norms that regulate political activity in the society. Thus, Lasswell might turn Easton's analysis around and show that the question of how political systems persist through change implies the question of who gets what, when, and how. This does not mean that Lasswell's query is more fundamental than Easton's, or the reverse. Instead, both theorists seem to be incorrect in their solutions to the problem of fundamentality. Looking back over the two arguments it appears that they mutually imply one another. Herbert Simon hinted at this solution when he remarked that the people with the most authority in an organization have the most influence in determining the content of decisional premises for others. However, he also observed that the authorities are limited by the overall purposes of the organization and the need to maintain cooperation. No conflict is unrestricted by some consensus on values and norms, and no agreement resolves all conflicts over the distribution of values. In other words, the problem of order implies the problem of distribution and the problem of distribution implies the problem of order.

Lasswell does not remain content to pose the question, Who gets what, when, and how? He breaks the basic question down into five "key questions" that define both his approach to political theory and his vision of the tasks of political science. Lasswell's listing of questions provides a convenient means of grasping the scope of political science: "What goal values are to be sought? What are the trends in the realization of values? What factors condition trends? What projections characterize the probable course of future developments? What policy alternatives will bring the greatest net realization of values?"[8]

Lasswell's first question—What goal values are to be sought in the political system (political life)?—is a query that has interested political theorists in the West since Plato presented speculations on the good political order. Essentially it is a question for prescriptive rather than descriptive political theorists. Usually the question is phrased: What values should be sought in the political system? Responses have ranged from the realization of love through the attainment of justice, to the maintenance of a minimum order. Most current political theorists of the behavioral persuasion are not explicitly concerned with the problem of what goals should be sought in the political system, although we have noted that many of them do make recommendations as an auxiliary activity.

Lasswell's second question—What are the trends in the realization of values in political systems?—is a query that has concerned generations of political historians in the West. For Lasswell, historians have been occupied with tracing out a map of who gets what, when and how over time. Where no written documents are available to aid in the determination of what values

---

[8] Lasswell, *Politics*, p. 187.

have been sought and how they have been distributed, the results of anthropological investigations into the cultures of preliterate societies are relevant. Political historians describe the rise and fall of elites that have obtained various goods through the use of a wide range of means. These historians are usually interested in providing detailed accounts of specific events and are not motivated to search systematically for generalizations about processes of social change that occur in societies far removed from one another in space and time. Lasswell believes that neither the question of the political philosopher—What values should be sought in the political system?—nor the question of the political historian—What are the trends in the realization of values in political systems?—are the proper questions for the political scientist or the political theorist of the behavioral persuasion to pose. Instead, he suggests that the key question for political scientists and behavioral theorists is, What factors condition trends in the realization of values in political systems? This query really represents a deepening of the question, Who gets what, when, and how? Lasswell proposes that political scientists and theorists investigate the conditions in which values are sought by political actors using a variety of methods. The problem is to determine first the conditions in which some values are sought rather than others. This first phase of investigation requires a theory that lists the basic values that can be sought in political systems over a wide range of space and time contexts. Lasswell has attempted to provide such a list of values. The second phase of investigation involves identifying the various types of political actors and stating the conditions that favor the emergence of some types rather than others. This part of political study requires a theory of the relationship between personality and politics, as well as a theory of stratification and the structure of elites. Lasswell's researches in psychiatry and personality theory and his study of Mosca's elite theory provided him with the concepts necessary to begin fulfillment of this requirement. The third part of the problem is determining the conditions in which some methods of gaining values are used rather than others. This phase of investigation requires a theory listing the various methods that have been used by political actors to attain values. This list of political methods must be capable of application over a wide range of space and time contexts. Lasswell's plan for political science and behavioral theory is ambitious, but it is not merely eclectic. While he pioneered in almost every important area of contemporary political theory and research, Lasswell also attempted to draw his investigations into a coherent whole. The extent of his success in this endeavor can be measured by the generality, logical interrelation and empirical relevance of the fundamental concepts defined in the *Politics*.

Lasswell's two final questions follow from the query, What factors condition trends in the realization of values in political systems? The question—What projections of trends in the realization of values characterize the probable course of future developments?—has attracted great prominence and interest among the students of futuristics or futurism in political science and other human studies. Scientifically grounded predictions of the future are, of course, dependent upon knowledge of the conditions in which particular values are sought by certain kinds of political actors employing specified means. When such knowledge is not available predictions can still be made, but they will have no scientific basis. Further, the predictions may even be correct. It is important to grasp the difference between scientific prediction and correct prediction. Scientific prediction is based on knowledge that when certain conditions have been present, certain events have occurred. A scientific prediction is phrased: If conditions x and y are present, event z will occur. Correct predictions may have a scientific basis, another basis or no consciously determinable basis at all. They are simply predictions that happen to have proven correct. At present scientifically grounded predictions of political events in human history can rarely be made. Most views of the future of politics are merely extensions of selected current trends. These are scientific predictions only in the most tenuous sense of the term. However, while political futuristics or political futurism may not be scientific pursuits, they may be useful. By depicting what might happen if selected trends are intensified, views of the political future may provide warnings of what actions to avoid. Lasswell believes that such projections of the future are important because all decisions in politics are based upon assumptions about the future. If these assumptions are brought into consciousness and questioned by being compared to alternative views of the future, more rational decisions, in Simon's sense of the term rationality, would be possible. This is the limited use of contemporary political futuristics.

Finally, Lasswell's fifth question—What policy alternatives will bring the greatest net realization of values in a political system?—also can only be answered scientifically after the conditions in which values are realized have been specified. One must know the full list of goals desired and the alternative means to reaching these goals. After such knowledge has been systematized, the most efficient means to attain ends can be recommended. It is important to note that the problem of how to attain the greatest net realization of values is always relative to an individual or group. The question really is what policy alternatives will bring the greatest net realization of values to a given actor or group of actors in a political system. "Policy science" or the scientifically grounded recommendation of means to attain given values can be used to aid dictators as well as democrats, revolutionaries as well as establishmentarians.

Through analyzing his basic question—Who gets what, when and how?— Lasswell has provided a set of requirements for basic theoretical categories and a vision of the tasks for political science. It is to the theoretical categories developed in the *Politics* that we now turn.

The Fundamental Concepts

In general terms Lasswell answers the question of who gets what, when and how with reference to the concept "elite." Lasswell remarks at the beginning of the *Politics* that the investigation of political activities is the inquiry into influence and the influential. Political scientists attempt to discover the conditions in which political actors attain values by using various means, while political philosophers try to justify the attainment of some values rather than others. For Lasswell, the influential are those "who get the most of what there is to get."[9] The influential make up the elite, and the people who do not receive a large proportion of socially available values comprise the mass. Thus, Lasswell does not define influence as in any way independent of the attainment of social values. Those human beings who attain the greatest share of values are influential, those who receive few goods are not. Frequently we think of influence as a relationship or a process through which values are attained, or as a resource, like money, that gives one a special advantage in gaining values. Lasswell does not use restricted definitions like these. He would say that all actions relevant to the attainment of values are part of the process of influence. Efficient use of violence, control of economic resources and manipulation of symbols are all modes of attaining values, or processes of influence. Even persuasion based on the appeal to scientific evidence and logical argumentation is a method of influencing decisions and attaining goals. While Lasswell would certainly recognize that there are differences between human relationships principled on force and human relationships principled on symbolic communication, he would call both types of relationships processes of influence as long as they were relevant to the attainment of values.

Lasswell would be in sharp disagreement with those who treat influence as a resource or as an attribute of human beings. Influence is the process of attaining values in which political actors engage, using a wide variety of means. Influence is not an object, like an automobile or a machine gun; it is the general political process. As we pointed out earlier, a political theorist is neither "right" nor "wrong" when he proposes a definition. Definitions are aids or impediments to solving problems (responding to questions) in specified areas of experience. Lasswell's definition of political science as the study of influence and his sweeping definition of influence imply that political scientists and theorists should carry their researches beyond the cross sections of activity that occur around governmental institutions and into all areas of social existence in which human beings compete for values. In the theories of Easton and Truman, activities became "political" or "politicized" when demands were made for allocations of value authoritative for an entire

---

[9] Lasswell, *Politics*, p. 13.

society. Lasswell's theory does not involve such a view of politics. Wherever the struggle for scarce values occurs political processes are present. Thus, Lasswell's theory allows for the study of academic politics, industrial politics and the politics of the family.

If the elite is that group of people in a society which appropriates the largest share of social values and the mass is that group of people in a society which is differentially deprived of social values, one problem for the political theorist is the definition of the possible social values that human beings can seek. In his original discussion in the *Politics* Lasswell listed three social values that can be the objects of influence processes. These values—deference, income and safety—correspond to the values of esteem, wealth and power that we discussed in connection with the political theories of Thomas Hobbes. In choosing these values Lasswell placed himself squarely in the tradition of modern political theory. However, in his later researches Lasswell found his original list of values inadequate in accounting for wide ranges of political activity. While he retained the values of power, wealth and respect (esteem), he added the values of well-being, rectitude, skill, enlightenment and affection to his list. Lasswell felt that this list exhausted the fundamental values that are sought in influence processes and also eliminated overlapping. The object of developing such a list, or typology, of values was to gain a means of comparing political activities over a wide range of space and time contexts.

By well-being Lasswell means health and comfort, and general biological values. The widespread concern with environmental pollution in industrialized societies illustrates how well-being can become an important social value. Neither power, wealth, nor respect is equivalent to well-being. Rectitude is essentially moral responsibility. To attain the value of rectitude one must be recognized as a person who adheres to certain standards of personal conduct. The importance of rectitude as a social value is illustrated by controversies over obscenity regulations and control, and periodic concern with corruption. By skill Lasswell means the ability to perform specialized tasks. The importance of skill in contemporary industrialized societies can hardly be overemphasized. Enlightenment is the possession and control of information. Deutsch's theory of politics as a communications process and Simon's view of organizational decision making as the determination of decisional premises illustrate the importance that the value of enlightenment has in contemporary societies. Continuing controversies over the control and content of the media of mass communications around the world give further evidence of the importance attached to "enlightenment." Finally, affection means the intimacy and warmth attached to close face-to-face relations, and the feelings of solidarity associated with the individual's identification with large groups. The existentialist description of contemporary human beings in industrialized societies as lonely, alone and lost, and the appearance in the twentieth century of mass emotional political movements, point up the continuing importance of affection as a value. Power, wealth, respect, well-being, rectitude, skill, enlightenment and affection are all values that may be sought in different ways by human beings.

In few societies does a single elite monopolize all of these values. In fact there may be built-in tensions and conflicts between some of the values. For example, to attain respect or deference, one may have to maintain a distance from others that prohibits the growth of relationships of affection. However, elites of power usually also attain great shares of one or more of the other values. Often they attain power just because they have these other values and can convert them into power. Whether or not Lasswell's list of values exhausts all of the major social values that can be sought by human beings, his typology is an improvement on the modern triad of power, wealth and respect.

Lasswell's list of values defines the "what" of politics. We remarked earlier that an adequate answer to the question of who gets what, when and how requires a list of the methods used in attaining values as well as a description of the values sought. In the *Politics* Lasswell provides such a typology of methods. He distinguishes among four general methods of attaining influence: symbol manipulation, application of violence, control of goods and patterning of institutional practices. Each one of these methods bears some discussion. Under symbol manipulation Lasswell includes forms of communication ranging from self-conscious propaganda to innocent espousals of the public good and the common destiny. Lasswell remarks that any "elite defends and asserts itself in the name of symbols of the common destiny."[10] Such symbol systems are ideologies when they are used to justify a governing elite and utopias when they are used in the campaign of a counter-elite to attain power. In a stable society attempts at self-conscious propaganda by reigning elites are relatively rare because the authorities have been able to mold the consciences of the people under their control. When counter-elites manipulate symbols they aim at destroying the efficacy of the norms of political obligation built into conscience. Lasswell makes the interesting point that because governing elites usually have superior access to the means of violence, economic goods and the institutional network, counter-elites are impelled to rely disproportionately on symbol manipulation to gain their objectives. In an era of revolution, specialists in symbol manipulation such as Lenin, Hitler, Mao and the media specialists active in American electoral campaigns have risen to prominence. The use of violence as a method of attaining influence is well known. Lasswell points out that in political

---

[10] Lasswell, *Politics*, p. 31.

contexts violence is usually expedient rather than sadistic. He remarks that the rational use of violence requires careful appraisal of its application in the context of its effects on the attainment of goals. The control of goods as a method of attaining influence is also well known. Governing elites use rationing and pricing to control behavior while counter-elites mobilize strikes and boycotts. Again Lasswell observes that the efficient use of economic tactics requires careful attention to a coherent strategy. Finally, the patterning of institutional practices as a means of attaining social values is familiar to anyone who has engaged in political and organizational activity. By practices Lasswell means "the ways by which elites are recruited and trained, all the forms observed in policy-making and administration."[11] Essentially, practices are rules of selection and decision. The ability to pattern them is itself a sign of influence, and the successful manipulation of institutional rules is in turn a source of influence in different spheres. As was the case with Lasswell's list of social values, the typology of means of gaining influence is an improvement over earlier modern views that equated politics and law with the application of coercion.

In addition to clarification of the "what" and "how" of politics, Lasswell provides some speculations on the relationships between politics and personality. In an attempt to get at the "who" of politics Lasswell proposes a major proposition about the psychological aspect of political activity. From Freudian personality theory Lasswell derived his famous principle that the political actor "displaces his private motives upon public objects, and rationalizes the displacement in terms of public advantage."[12] By this statement Lasswell means that in early childhood individuals experience some frustration in getting their needs satisfied. When such frustrations are not consciously managed the desires may remain active, but unconscious, and may lead the individual to attempt to satisfy them indirectly. For example, a man deprived of affection in early childhood may seek adulation by becoming an agitator as an adult. This simplified explanation does not do justice to the complexities and problems involved in serious depth analysis of political actors. Psychoanalytic descriptions have become popular means to discrediting and ridiculing political and social opponents. They usually have no scientific standing in such contexts and should be discounted. Lasswell himself resorted to oversimplification in his formula that politicians displace private motives on public objects.

Lasswell's political theory contains responses to the questions, Who? (elites and certain personality types), What? (the values of power, wealth, respect, well-being, rectitude, skill, enlightenment and affection), How? (symbol manipulation, application of violence, control of goods and patterning of

---

[11] Lasswell, *Politics*, p. 80.
[12] Lasswell, *Politics*, p. 133.

practices). The theory contains few answers to the question, When? or, Under what conditions do particular elites seek certain values using specific means? Thus, Lasswell has developed a set of theoretical categories with few conditional relationships among them. This is the case for most current political theories.

Imaginative Perspective

In Lasswell's political world it is vital to understand what social values are deemed most significant. Lasswell believes that the value of skill is becoming the most important in the contemporary world. While modern political systems have been controlled by elites of wealth, the next great revolution in the West will witness the ascendancy of elites of skill. In contrast to popular nightmarish visions of a civil war between the men of specialized knowledge and the useless and obsolescent, Lasswell projects a vision of a mass movement uniting all people who have sacrificed to gain a socially useful skill from skilled blue collar workers to professionals. This coalition would demand just recompense for social contribution and would displace elites of ownership. Lasswell articulated this projection in 1936. Since that time intellectuals have become much more pessimistic. The horrors of World War II, the fear of nuclear destruction, the Cold War and increasing militarization throughout the world dimmed hopes for a coalition of the skilled. Adolf Eichmann, skilled in transportation management, placed himself at the service of a regime that perverted his skills. Even Lasswell's fervor dimmed during the war. He wrote an essay called "The Garrison State" in which he predicted that Western societies would become great barracks.[13] The specialists in violence rather than the skilled would reign. However, Lasswell's emphasis on the importance of stratification by skill is shared by many current political theorists. They just do not view the increasing relevance of skill as an unmixed blessing and they hardly ever mention a coalition of reform based on skill. What values are regnant in contemporary Western societies? What values might be stressed by counter-elites? What kind of coalition of reform is currently possible? These are the kinds of questions that Lasswell's theory provokes for the citizen.

Robert A. Dahl

Robert A. Dahl is one of the most important theorists of political pluralism in the United States. While Harold Lasswell's work has been directed toward

---

[13] Harold D. Lasswell, "The Garrison State," *The Analysis of Political Behaviour: An Empirical Approach* (London: Routledge and Kegan Paul, 1948).

furthering the study of political elites, Dahl has argued that the idea that contemporary democratic societies are ruled by a single governing elite is incorrect. Both Lasswell and Dahl have been occupied with describing the distribution and dynamics of political influence. Lasswell believes that in all complex societies influence is concentrated in a particular stratum of people. Dahl maintains that in contemporary representative democracies influence is dispersed among many diverse interest groups. Groups that are successful in realizing their policy preferences on some issues are likely to fail to get their way on other issues. Lasswell's idea that influence is concentrated identifies him as an elite theorist and Dahl's notion that influence is dispersed identifies him as a pluralist.

It is important to remember that the debate between elite and pluralist political theorists does not concern disagreement about the fundamental problem that political theorists should study. "Who gets what, when and how?" is the basic question that both Dahl and Lasswell seek to answer. Rather, elite and pluralist political theorists differ on the answer to the question of influence. Thus, this disagreement is often expressed as a debate about how to study influence rather than as a debate over the appropriate concepts with which to describe political events. In other words, the disputes between elite and pluralist political theorists are often methodological rather than theoretical. In contrast, disagreements between systems theorists who ask—How do political systems persist through change?—and influence theorists who ask—Who gets what, when and how?—are mainly theoretical rather than methodological.

Robert Dahl's interest in the distribution of influence in contemporary democracies has been expressed in several volumes. In *A Preface to Democratic Theory,* Dahl undertook a philosophical analysis of the different conceptions of democracy that he found to be important in American history.[14] In this book he uncovered logical contradictions in the conceptions of Madisonian democracy and populist democracy, and suggested a model of democracy that he called polyarchy to guide empirical research into American institutions. In *Who Governs?* Dahl both tested his notion of polyarchy against observations of political events in New Haven, Connecticut, and further refined his theory of the distribution of influence in the American political system.[15] *Who Governs?* presents the most ambitious challenge to elite theory available in the literature of American political science. Dahl has continued his studies of influence in his text *Pluralist Democracy in the United States,* which applies the propositions developed in *Who Governs?* to a

---

[14] Robert A. Dahl, *A Preface to Democratic Theory* (Chicago: University of Chicago Press, 1956).

[15] Robert A. Dahl, *Who Governs?* (New Haven: Yale University Press, 1961).

wider context.[16] In our discussion of Dahl's pluralist theory of politics we will rely primarily on the questions posed and the concepts defined in *Who Governs?*

The Political Question

Like Lasswell, Dahl states his basic question in the title of his most famous book. He explains that his task is to approach the ancient question of political rule by examining the politics of a New England city. He phrases his basic question with particular reference to democratic political systems: "In a political system where nearly every adult may vote but where knowledge, wealth, social position, access to officials, and other resources are unequally distributed, who actually governs?"[17] While Dahl's question might appear at first to be simpler than Lasswell's, it actually conceals a great deal of complexity. If one wishes to answer the question—Who governs?—one must know what governance means. On the one hand, the governors cannot be identified with those who occupy official positions because Dahl is concerned with describing actual processes of influence rather than legal structures. On the other hand, the governors cannot be identified with those people who have acquired the most knowledge, wealth, social position, access to officials and other resources, because it is the use of these resources rather than their concentration that constitutes governance. Here Dahl diverges from Lasswell who identified the elite as those people who attained the greatest share of socially available values. For Lasswell, the attainment of value was the most dependable sign of influence. Dahl has a much more subtle view of influence. Essentially, he holds that the greater the share that one has in determining the content and enforcement of decisions, the greater the influence that one possesses. Thus, Dahl, like Simon, views political processes as decision-making processes.

Dahl sketches several possible answers to the question, Who governs? He notes that one familiar answer states that in contemporary representative democracies competing political parties govern with the consent of the electorate. This is the answer that people learn in most high school civics courses. The argument has two versions. In the first version, competitive parties contest elections by offering divergent programs for solving public problems. From among these programs voters choose the policies that they deem the most desirable and vote for the party representing these policies. The party that is elected is responsible for carrying out its campaign promises

---

[16]Robert A. Dahl, *Pluralist Democracy in the United States* (Chicago: Rand-McNally Book Co., 1967).
[17]Robert A. Dahl, *Who Governs?*, p. 1.

as far as possible. It is held accountable for its actions at the subsequent election. In the second version of the argument that political parties govern in contemporary representative democracies, competitive parties contest elections by offering candidates to the electorate. From among these candidates voters choose the people in whom they are willing to place their trust. Since the important public issues in complex societies are technical and difficult to understand parties are held accountable for their general performance rather than for the fulfillment of specific promises. Even if the voters cannot understand the intricacies of contemporary policy making, they can judge whether or not the "shoe pinches." If it pinches enough they will choose a new leadership at the next election. Dahl dismisses the view that parties govern in contemporary representative democracies with very little discussion. In the United States, national parties are characterized by severe divisions among leaders on significant issues. Also, the view that parties govern ignores the many access points to the decision-making process throughout the political system. Attention to these access points was David Truman's major contribution to current political theory.

A second answer to the question of who governs follows from the perspective of interest group theory. Here one argues that behind the façade of party government are innumerable activities of interest groups. Political interest groups, pressing their demands upon other social groups for resources and actions through the government, rule in contemporary representative democracies. The activities of political parties represent merely a summing up of many cross sections of interest group behavior. We have noted that interest group theories of politics, such as David Truman's, are consistent with the systems theories of politics that are dominant in contemporary American political science. Dahl does not dismiss the interest group interpretation of American politics. His own theory is an attempt to supplement interest group theory with a theory of political leadership.

A third answer to the question stresses the role of elites. In this case one argues that social and economic elites govern, regardless of whether the formal political system, or constitution, is democratic, fascist, communist or some other. In the *Politics* Lasswell presented the standard argument in support of the elitist interpretation of political influence. In every complex society there are significant inequalities in the distribution of socially available values. Most people would like to increase their share of socially available values. Political activity is one means through which a greater share of socially available values can be obtained. Those who already are favored by the system of distribution in a society will tend to use political activity to prevent the less fortunate from increasing their share and to extend their own acquisitions. Social and economic elites will employ violence, organized economic sanctions and symbol manipulation to further their purposes in the political system and, thus, will become political elites. Dahl maintains that the argument of elite theorists must be taken seriously, but must not be assumed as a postulate. He holds that most elite theorists have been so convinced that social and economic elites govern that no evidence to the contrary could shake their faith. He views his study of influence in New Haven as a first step toward testing the proposition that social and economic elites govern in contemporary representative democracies.

Dahl criticizes the views that parties, interest groups and elites govern on the grounds that none of these explanations take account of the role of politicians in politics. In the three interpretations that we have discussed politicians were merely agents for the majority, the party, interest groups or the elite. Dahl observes that there is an old tradition in political studies that emphasizes the importance of political leadership in the decision-making process. This tradition, which goes back at least as far as the writing of Machiavelli, is congenial to Dahl's point of view. Dahl asserts that in his tradition of political studies "majorities, parties, interest groups, elites, even political systems are all to some extent pliable; a leader who knows how to use his resources to the maximum is not so much the agent of others as others are his agents."[18] Thus, Dahl's pluralism is essentially a theory of political leadership. He shifts the emphasis from Lasswell's concern with the distribution of values to the processes through which decisions are made and values are allocated. He is primarily interested in the mobilization of influence and the ways in which actors use their political resources.

Having criticized the theories of party government, interest group politics and elites, Dahl analyzes a fourth answer to the question, Who governs? Here one argues that neither the people nor the elites govern, but both. In contemporary societies people are detached from traditional relations and become members of rootless masses. Demagogic leaders appeal to the base desires of these masses and employ the support they receive to obliterate opposition to their rule. The result is a totalitarian state. According to this "mass society" theory of contemporary politics, all current industrialized societies have important aspects of totalitarianism. Dahl agrees with the mass society theorists that both leaders and constituents govern in contemporary representative democracies, but he maintains that people in the modern world are not organized into masses. Instead, he holds that representative democracies in the modern world are associated with multi-group societies. Political leaders in the United States do not confront rootless masses whose directions change with each shift in the winds of doctrine. They enter into successive relationships with various groups, each of which has some relatively permanent interest or situation. Despite his disagreement with mass society

---

[18] Robert A. Dahl, *Who Governs?*, p. 6.

theory, Dahl analyzes it seriously. As in the case of his critique of elite theory, he does not declare that the propositions of mass society theorists are absurd or meaningless. He is ready to test them against the political events he observes in New Haven, but he criticizes people who assume that they are true regardless of the outcome of observation.

Dahl's review of the standard responses to the question of who governs convinces him that the query should be divided into several parts. He finds that a problem with elite theory is the assumption that political resources are cumulative. Dahl claims that elite theorists, like Lasswell, assume that people who have a large share of some social or economic value also have a large share of influence. He would like to challenge this assumption and, thus, he poses the question: "Are inequalities in resources of influence 'cumulative' or 'noncumulative'?"[19] Dahl also challenges other assumptions that he believes have characterized elite theories of politics. Instead of assuming that decisions are made in accordance with the dictates of the socially and economically privileged, he will investigate how political decisions are actually made. Rather than assuming that the same group of people is most influential in making all significant political decisions, he will investigate who gets what, when and how on specific issues. Instead of assuming that social and economic elites are unified in viewpoint and interest, he will investigate the patterns of consensus and conflict among the privileged. Rather than assuming that the vote is a meaningless procedure in contemporary representative democracies, Dahl will study the responsiveness of political leaders to different groups of citizens. Instead of assuming that social and economic elites attempt to block change in social structures, Dahl will try to discover the sources of stability and change in the political system. Finally, rather than assuming that the democratic creed represents elite propaganda, Dahl will investigate the degree to which political decisions are affected by democratic beliefs. The set of queries derived from the basic question—Who governs?—creates a difficult task for Dahl. The techniques for discovering the distribution of influence among various political actors have not been perfected. Dahl's responses to his questions must be judged as very tentative. Bearing this in mind, we may turn to Dahl's description of a pluralist democracy.

The Fundamental Concepts

Dahl's basic thesis about the distribution of influence in New Haven is that over the past century and a half the distribution of influence has changed from organization into cumulative inequalities to organization into dispersed inequalities. By cumulative inequality Dahl means that if a person or group

---

[19] Robert A. Dahl, *Who Governs?*, p. 7.

has privileged access to one socially available value, that person or group is likely to have privileged access to other socially available values. By dispersed inequality Dahl means that if a person or group has privileged access to one socially available value, that person or group is not likely to have privileged access to other socially available values. Thus, in expressing his basic thesis Dahl denies the claims of both elite theorists and mass society theorists. The elite theorists believe that inequalities are always cumulative, and usually hold that economic privileges are the foundation for social and political privileges. The mass society theorists believe that in contemporary industrialized societies inequalities are cumulative, and frequently hold that political privileges are the foundation for social and economic privileges.

Dahl notes that there have been three distinct periods in the political history of New Haven. Between the end of the eighteenth century and the beginning of the nineteenth century the "patricians" governed. The patricians were members of the Anglo-Saxon and Puritan aristocracy that had first colonized Connecticut and the rest of New England. The patricians were favored by a situation of cumulative inequalities. They were members of an economic elite that owned the commercial and trading establishments that dominated the Connecticut economy. The patricians also formed a social elite that could claim the deference of other residents of New Haven. As an important feature of their social ascendancy, the patricians controlled the important religious organizations in Connecticut. Dahl believes that this religious ascendancy may have been the most important aspect of the patricians' power because of the theocratic emphasis of New England society in the early nineteenth century. Finally, the patricians were members of a political elite that essentially monopolized the important public offices in New Haven until 1850.

By 1850 important changes had occurred in the economy of New Haven as well as in the economy of the United States. Industrialization brought a new set of people, the entrepreneurs, into prominence. While the patricians had the economic resources to organize the new industries, they did not have the will to become industrialists. They left the task of industrial organization to the new class of entrepreneurs whose members often came from middle, lower-middle or working class backgrounds. Dahl notes that the emergence of the entrepreneurs signalled a partial breakdown of the system of cumulative inequalities that had favored the patricians. While the entrepreneurs eventually came to dominate the economic system of New Haven, the patricians would not accord them social privileges. Thus, the hierarchies of wealth and deference were controlled by different groups. In the political system, the entrepreneurs were able to break the ascendancy of the patricians and ultimately displace them. From the middle of the nineteenth century until the beginning of the twentieth century entrepreneurs, the owners and organizers of large businesses, monopolized the important public offices in New Haven.

The era of entrepreneurial dominance was a transitional period between situations of cumulative inequalities of resources and values and dispersed inequalities of resources and values. By 1900 the entrepreneurs had created a group of people who could effectively challenge their political domination. In search of a labor force to tend the machines in their factories the entrepreneurs encouraged the immigration of people from central, southern and eastern Europe. These people did not share the New England culture of the patricians and the entrepreneurs, and they had little hope of organizing large industries. However, once they became citizens they did acquire the vote and they could use it to elect candidates who might protect their interests. Dahl remarks that the immigrants chose a politics of assimilation rather than a politics of reform. They did not ask so much for a collective redistribution of social and economic resources as they demanded opportunities to become Americanized and eventually middle class. Instead of surmounting the barriers created by their nationalities and forming a grand coalition of immigrant workers to do battle with the entrepreneurs, they formed economic alliances in the labor unions and entered politics through their specific nationality, or ethnic, groups.

The political activities of the ethnic groups were responsible for the emergence of a new set of leaders, the ex-plebes. The ex-plebes were members of ethnic groups who entered local politics through the Democratic or Republican parties and served as representatives of their groups. The rise of the ex-plebes in the political system provoked another breakdown of cumulative inequalities. While economic and political privilege had been split off from social privilege with the ascendancy of the entrepreneurs, the rise of the ex-plebes brought about a split of economic privilege and political privilege. While the entrepreneurs, or their successors in the managements of large national corporations, continued to dominate the economic hierarchy, the ex-plebes more and more gained control over the important public offices in New Haven.

The history of political rule in New Haven does not end with the rise of the ex-plebes. Dahl notes that a change has been occurring in the pattern of New Haven politics since World War II. He remarks that the political dominance of the ex-plebes completed the transition from cumulative inequalities to dispersed inequalities: "What the immigrants and the ex-plebes had accomplished, however, was a further split in political resources. Popularity had been split off from both wealth and social standing. Popularity meant votes; votes meant office; office meant influence."[20] However, once the ethnic

---

[20] Robert A. Dahl, *Who Governs?*, p. 51.

groups had been successful in realizing their goal of assimilation into American society, politics could no longer be based on the issues of assimilation. Dahl observes that by the middle of the twentieth century demands were forming for new benefits from the political system. Dahl notes that the benefits that people and groups demand from the political system may be either divisible or indivisible. Divisible benefits can be given to specific individuals. For example, when a politician could offer one of his constituents a government job he would be dispensing a divisible benefit. Dahl maintains that in the ethnic politics of the ex-plebes political leaders would offer divisible benefits to their constituents in accordance with an ethnic criterion. Indivisible benefits cannot be portioned out to specific people, but affect an entire community. For example, a system for controlling water pollution would benefit everyone in a community. Dahl holds that there has been a shift in the political demands in New Haven from appeals for divisible benefits to appeals for indivisible benefits. He remarks that there is a new emphasis on benefits from the political system that go to citizens in general rather than to specific individuals or groups. Dahl expects a new class of political leaders to emerge. These leaders, the "new men," may "very well prove to be the bureaucrats and experts—and politicians who know how to use them."[21] Like Lasswell, Dahl is impressed by the importance of skill in contemporary industrialized societies. Dahl is not prepared to comment about whether or not the new demand for indivisible goods and the attendant need for expert skills in government and society in general will lead to an era in which cumulative inequalities again characterize the social system. Perhaps the resource of technical skill will further disperse influence, creating a new group to stand beside the social elect, the economically powerful and the popular. However, it is also possible that the experts and the managers will coalesce into a homogeneous class that is set off in interest and privilege from the rest of the people who do not have specialized skills. If this kind of division occurs, the nightmare of a civil war between the enlightened and the benighted will be more than a frightening scenario.

Our discussion of Dahl's interpretation of the political history of New Haven has more than passing significance. It is a concrete illustration of the point that pluralist political theory does not differ from the theory of political elites in either the fundamental question that it poses or the basic concepts that characterize it. Dahl recognized the presence of a political elite dependent on a system of cumulative inequalities in New Haven. Between the end of the eighteenth century and the middle of the nineteenth century the patricians formed a social, economic and political elite. However, Dahl argued that this elite lost its economic and political ascendancy because of changes in

---

[21] Robert A. Dahl, *Who Governs?*, p. 62.

the economy. Thus, Dahl does not claim that pluralism, or a system of dispersed inequalities, must characterize every social system. He maintains that influence will be exercised in every political system, but that it is a matter of empirical testing whether or not an elite is in control.

We noted earlier that disagreements between elite and pluralist political theorists are usually expressed as debates about how to study influence rather than as debates over the appropriate concepts with which to describe political events. This pattern of dispute occurs because elite and pluralist political theorists differ on the answer to the question of who governs rather than on the merits of posing that question. Dahl studied the distribution of influence in New Haven by investigating the way decisions were made on three presumably basic issues: party nominations for the mayoralty, urban redevelopment and education. The first issue was chosen because it defined influence in the formal governmental structure, and the second two issues were chosen because of the large amount of economic resources involved in their settlement. Dahl found that a small group of professional politicians, the ex-plebes, decided upon nominations for mayor, that businessmen were more influential in the area of urban redevelopment and that groups involved in the educational bureaucracy had significant influence in the area of education. Dahl also found that the mayor was the only person who had significant influence in all of the three issue-areas. It was through his close study of decisions on these three issues that Dahl arrived at his conclusion that the politics of New Haven was characterized by dispersed inequalities of influence.

Dahl's study has been criticized on many grounds. One might object that even if Dahl is correct about the distribution of influence in New Haven, his findings have little relevance for the distribution of influence in the United States or even in other American cities. Further, one might argue that basic decisions are made at other levels than the local community, and that local political decisions are limited by allocations of values that have been made by the federal government, national business corporations and other bureaucracies. Finally, one might argue that local political decisions are limited by norms and values that have been socialized into political actors. If these norms and values favor the interests of socially and economically privileged groups, these groups have no reason to act overtly in politics. The first objection is methodological and has to do with the degree to which Dahl's findings can be generalized. The second objection would be made by an elite theorist like Lasswell who would contend that as long as the elite controls the commanding heights of power it can leave localities a small measure of autonomy. The third objection would be made by a systems theorist who would claim that one must look behind the surface conflicts of political life to the norms that limit conflict. An examination of these norms, which most citizens take for granted, may reveal biases that favor the interests of some groups over others.

Imaginative Perspective

Dahl applies his theory of dispersed inequalities to a description of the political life of the individual in the United States. He distinguishes between two types of people, *homo civicus* and *homo politicus*. Civic man, simply the normal human being, nas few interests in politics. He is usually involved with his work, his family life and recreation, and normally enters the political system only to cast a ballot. Political man makes a vocation out of politics and devotes large portions of his time and effort to political activity. Political man has a fairly wide area for maneuver in the political arena just because civic man usually does not use all of the political resources at his disposal. *Homo civicus* will begin to use his resources only when his core interests at work or at home are threatened. When these interests are threatened he may mobilize with other people of like interest and press demands through an interest group. It is the possibility of such mobilization that restrains *homo politicus* from becoming the dictator pictured in mass society theories of politics. Dahl's perspective on politics implies that it would be dangerous for the stability of the system of dispersed inequalities if most people participated in politics when their immediate interests were not threatened. More and more people are challenging this implication as public problems like pollution of the environment, foreign policy and defense become prominent. The growing preoccupation with collective benefits may challenge the privatization of *homo civicus*. It is ironic that Dahl, who noted a shift in concern from divisible to indivisible benefits, did not recognize how this might threaten the traditional division between civic man and political man.

Theories of Contemporary Democracy

5

One of the major objectives of many current political theorists of the behavioral persuasion was to generalize knowledge about political affairs beyond statements concerning particular political systems. David Easton, in *A Systems Analysis of Political Life,* explicitly maintained that political theorists should attempt to identify units of analysis that could be applied to the study of any political system. Theorists of political subsystems like Herbert A. Simon and Peter Blau tried to be even more general in their approaches. Their theories of organization were meant to apply to the dynamics of bureaucracies and other associations, as well as to the processes of governments. Theorists of political influence, particularly theorists of political elites like Harold Lasswell, similarly attempted to generalize beyond specific political systems. They believed that the struggle for influence was universal and that it was carried on through essentially the same methods everywhere. Just this interest in generalization and abstraction by theorists of political systems, political subsystems and political influence has been criticized by many academic opponents of current theorists of the behavioral persuasion. These critics insist that one cannot apply the same concepts in the analysis of democratic regimes and totalitarian dictatorships without losing significant information. Whether or not this criticism is well-taken depends upon what kind of information one considers significant. If one is interested in the features that characterize all political systems, there should be no *a priori* complaint against general theories of political systems, subsystems and influence. If one is concerned with the features that characterize certain types of political systems, or specific regimes, there should be no *a priori* complaint against specialized theories meant to illuminate these features.

Without repudiating the goal of a general theory of political activity, a group of current theorists of the behavioral persuasion has fixed attention upon the conditions in which democratic political systems are most likely to emerge and persist. These theorists do not maintain that they have developed approaches that utilize unique concepts. They do not hold that one set of units of analysis can be applied to the study of democracies, another set to the study of dictatorships and still another set to the investigation of political systems in general. They employ many of the concepts that the general theorists use. For example, Gabriel Almond and Sidney Verba, who explore the attitudes that sustain democratic regimes, use Easton's ideas of demand, input and output as their theoretical framework. Seymour M. Lipset, who investigates the social factors that sustain democratic regimes, employs Truman's notion of multiple memberships and cross-cutting group affiliations as a key explanatory concept. Thus, current theorists of the behavioral persuasion who explore the social and psychological conditions for democracy are not outside of the mainstream of contemporary empirical theory. They apply the same kinds of concepts as other theorists do, but to a special problem. For example, a theorist applying Harold Lasswell's theory of political elites to the study of modern democracy would be interested in finding out the frequency and situations in which the methods of symbol manipulation, economic power and violence were used in democracies. Perhaps after discovering the frequencies and contexts he would be concerned with comparing them to the patterns observed in other systems.

The reasons many current theorists of the behavioral persuasion decided to study the conditions in which democratic regimes persist go beyond the internal development of political science. Two events that occurred after World War II convinced many theorists to study democracy. First, the Cold War between the Western representative democracies and the communist world drove some theorists to explore the factors that favored apparent stability and freedom in the West. Second, the breakdown of colonialism and the emergence of new nations around the world posed the question of what kind of political systems these emerging nations would adopt.

This question was uppermost in the minds of both Seymour M. Lipset and Gabriel Almond. They felt that the Soviet Union offered the emerging nations an appealing model for rapid economic development through forced savings and forced industrialization. That model was particularly appealing because it was different from the capitalist model long associated with imperialism and colonialism. However, the Soviet example had the drawback of requiring a repressive political system. Both Lipset and Almond were concerned with the problem of whether political democracy would be possible in emerging nations committed to rapid economic development. They felt that a study of the conditions in which democracy was sustained in the West would be helpful in determining whether democracy was possible in the new nations. In their conclusions they dissociated political democracy from the economics of capitalism, but they were not optimistic about the early appearance of democracy in the emerging nations. Almond argued that while the new nations could adopt the familiar Western democratic institutions like popular elections, political parties, legislatures and courts, the people in these nations could not easily learn the subtle attitudes that sustained democracy in countries like the United States and Great Britain. Lipset maintained that the chances for stable democracy were not good where a high standard of living did not exist. Thus, the attempt to find out whether democracy was possible in the new nations ended in frustration. While traditional capitalism was not a condition of democracy, other socioeconomic and cultural conditions that were lacking in the emerging nations seemed to be prerequisites.

Of course, there were also reasons for studying the conditions of democracy that were derived from the internal development of political science. During and immediately following World War II sociologists and social psychologists began seriously studying the social and psychological factors involved in electoral decision making. The voting studies, which contained correlations of the voting decision with the social and psychological characteristics of individuals, cast doubt on some of the traditional assumptions of democratic theory. Gabriel Almond and Sidney Verba have called the classical democratic theory the "rationality-activist" model of political culture. According to the "rationality-activist" model, the democratic citizen is expected to be very active and involved in politics. Further, the democratic citizen is supposed to be guided by reason rather than by emotion in his approach to politics. Finally, the democratic citizen "is supposed to be well informed and to make decisions—for instance, his decision on how to vote—on the basis of careful calculation as to the interests and the principles he would like to see furthered."[1] If the voting studies are correct, and there is no reason to question their accuracy, none of the conditions of the "rationality-activist" model of democratic politics is met in contemporary Western representative democracies.

Large numbers of people in countries like the United States show little or no interest in political affairs. We have seen that Robert Dahl believes that such political apathy reduces political conflict and, therefore, aids the stability of the political system. Almond and Verba advance much the same argument. Few people in Western representative democracies consider political issues in a fully rational way. They do not vote after a careful consideration of how their action can be an efficient means to attain their goals.

---

[1] Gabriel A. Almond and Sidney Verba, *The Civic Culture* (Boston: Little, Brown and Company, 1965), p. 29.

There is some question about whether many people would vote at all if they made such a serious consideration and calculation. Finally, few people in Western representative democracies are well informed about local, national and international political issues. Even if they attempted to make their vote an efficient means to some goal, the voting studies show that they would not have the knowledge necessary to make such a rational calculation. Few people are willing to spend the time necessary to learn about the substance of political issues and the ways in which they can participate in political activity.

The attack on the "rationality-activist" model of democracy by sociologists and social psychologists drove some current political theorists to reexamine democratic political systems. If most people were not good citizens according to the standards of classical democratic theory, how did Western representative democracies work? We have already discussed some of the responses to this question under the headings of theories of political subsystems and theories of political influence. David Truman argued that American democracy was sustained by a widespread agreement on the limits of legitimate political activity and widespread multiple memberships of individuals in competing interest groups. While the vote in a Western democracy might not determine all significant matters of policy, the conflict among interest groups, blunted by consensus on the "rules of the game" and multiple memberships, favored an open and a free society. Robert Dahl maintained that American democracy was characterized by a system of dispersed inequalities of power. Various groups and individuals have significant influence in particular "issue-areas" that directly concern their life situations. They probably have little influence over decisions that do not affect their immediate working conditions and family situations. For Dahl, a relatively open and free society is maintained by this system of dispersed inequalities of power. The theorists considered in this section, Seymour M. Lipset, Gabriel Almond and Sidney Verba, follow closely the approaches of Truman and Dahl. Lipset's work has much in common with Truman's presentation, while Almond's and Verba's analysis is much like Dahl's.

The Political Question

Current theorists of the behavioral persuasion were interested in more than merely describing how Western representative democracies function in the absence of an enlightened body of citizens. They were primarily concerned with discovering the conditions in which democratic institutions appear and persist. Generally, there are two approaches to responding to the question, What are the conditions that sustain representative democracies? First, one may attempt to discover the social and economic conditions that are associated with the appearance of political institutions. This is the approach of

Lipset, who investigates the "social bases" of democracy. He finds that democracies are sustained by high levels of economic development. Second, one may attempt to discover the cultural and social psychological conditions that are associated with the appearance of political institutions. This is the approach of Almond and Verba, who investigate the configuration of political attitudes in contemporary democracies. They find that democracies are sustained by feelings of trust and allegiance.

There are also two general ways of defining democracy. First, one may define democracy as a set of formal institutions, such as competitive parties and a system of majority rule. Lipset takes this approach. Second, one may define democracy as Truman and Dahl have described the pluralist commonwealth. Almond and Verba follow this approach. In either case the democratic political system is the phenomenon to be explained. The social bases and the cultural and social psychological configurations are the explanatory variables.

It is likely that neither the socioeconomic analysis of Lipset nor Almond's and Verba's cultural and social psychological approach is adequate to account for the appearance and persistence of democratic political systems. In his discussion of social causation, Lipset has presented a view that is sounder than the conception of one-way dependence of political phenomena on some other factors. Lipset claims that complex systems like political democracies have multi-variate causation and consequences. By multi-variate causation Lipset means that a wide range and large number of conditions are involved in the appearance and maintenance of political systems. By multi-variate consequences, Lipset means that political systems have a wide range and large number of effects on other systems and even on themselves. Some of these effects may further sustain the system, while others may tend to break it down. The fact that political systems can produce consequences that affect their own persistence removes them from complete dependence on socioeconomic or cultural and social psychological conditions. The idea of multi-variate consequences is contained in the notion of Easton and Deutsch that feedback is a crucial process in political systems. The outputs of a political system never become fully divorced from the future states of that system. Thus, as long as a political system has some control over the demands that it processes, it has an independent sphere of causation. Current theorists of the behavioral persuasion who have studied the conditions for democracy have shown that no one zone of human activity fully determines another.

Seymour Martin Lipset

Current political theories of the behavioral persuasion have been heavily influenced by the conceptual frameworks and research projects developed by sociologists. The first large-scale empirical research projects that investigated political behavior were the voting studies conducted by sociologists and social psychologists. Bernard Berelson, Paul F. Lazarsfeld and William McPhee pioneered in the field of survey research into the attitudes of voters.[2] Originally they were less interested in accounting for specifically political behavior than they were concerned with investigating the bases of human choice. The act of voting provided a convenient decisional situation for study. After World War II political scientists discovered the work that sociologists like Lazarsfeld had been perfecting. They began to apply the techniques of questionnaire research to problems of political behavior. At the same time that research into voting behavior was becoming important in sociology and political science, sociological theorists like Talcott Parsons and Robert Merton were elaborating systems theories of society. Peter Blau, whom we discussed under the heading of organization theory, was one of Robert Merton's students. The other current theories of political systems and sub-systems that we have analyzed were greatly influenced by the theories of Parsons and Merton. The research into voting behavior and political attitudes, and the construction of theories of the social system by sociologists, have not merely influenced the work of contemporary political scientists. In the discipline of sociology, the important subfield of political sociology has emerged. The differences between the research of political sociologists and political scientists are minimal, if they exist at all. Political scientists and political sociologists use the same research methods and explore the same problems. Along with the growth of political sociology as a subfield has come the development of theories of the behavioral persuasion. These theories are quite similar to those elaborated on by political scientists.

Perhaps the scholar who best represents the two traditions of voting analysis and systems theories of society characterizing political sociology is Seymour Martin Lipset. Lipset's work has been nearly as wide-ranging as Harold Lasswell's. He is one of the pioneers in the study of the politics of "private governments," such as labor unions and other voluntary organizations. His study of the politics of the International Typographical Union, undertaken with Martin Trow and James S. Coleman, has become a classic example of "deviant case analysis."[3] Lipset and his collaborators studied the ITU because it was characterized by a competitive two-party political system while most unions were characterized by one-party systems. Through a close analysis of the ITU they found many factors in its membership and history that helped explain why its political system approximated a two-party

---

[2] Bernard Berelson, Paul F. Lazarsfeld and William McPhee, *Voting* (Chicago: University of Chicago Press, 1954).
[3] S. M. Lipset, M. Trow, and J. S. Coleman, *Union Democracy* (Glencoe: The Free Press, 1956).

democracy. These factors were not present in the history and membership of other American labor unions. Thus, by treating the ITU as a deviant case of labor union politics, Lipset and his collaborators were able to develop a theory that listed the conditions in which labor unions and, by implication, other voluntary organizations, were most likely to have competitive two-party political systems.

Lipset has also devoted a great deal of attention to voting behavior in the West. In *Political Man* he has analyzed a large number of voting studies with the aim of deriving generalizations from them about the structural conditions that might account for diverse voting patterns.[4] Perhaps the most interesting work that Lipset has done, however, is his analysis of the conditions that favor the appearance of political democracies on the level of the nation state. Again, in *Political Man* he has developed a theory of the social conditions present in contemporary democracies. Lipset's discussion of democracy in nation states is continuous with his discussion of democracy in private governments, such as labor unions. Thus, Lipset is one of the few theorists who have actually attempted to bridge the gap between organization theories and political theories. He has been aided in this effort of synthesis by the strategy of uniting diverse levels of analysis through the investigation of a specific political process. A concern with competitive two-party and multi-party democracies has unified Lipset's theoretical and research activities. Lipset's interests have not been exhausted by the theoretical problems of democracy and the research problems of voting behavior. He has also worked in the intermediate zone of the analysis of political ideologies and political history. Finally, he has devoted attention to the history of social thought. In our discussion of Lipset's political theory we will be primarily concerned with the questions posed and the concepts elaborated on in *Political Man.*

The Political Question

Like most current political theorists, Lipset is clear about the basic question that he poses in his work. He states that he is primarily concerned with democracy as a characteristic of social systems and that the principal topics that interest him are "the conditions necessary for democracy in societies and organizations; the factors which affect men's participation in politics, particularly their behavior as voters; and the sources of support for values and movements which sustain or threaten democratic institutions."[5] Thus, we might phrase Lipset's basic question as, How do democratic political systems persist through stressful change? This way of putting the question forges a connecting link between Lipset's concerns and those of the theorists of

---

[4]Seymour Martin Lipset, *Political Man* (Garden City: Doubleday and Co., 1963).
[5]Lipset, *Political Man,* p. x.

political systems and subsystems. Under this interpretation, Lipset's theory would merely be a specialized variety of systems theory. Rather than presenting a general theory of all political systems, he would be developing a special theory of democratic political systems. We would expect Lipset to list the norms and values most favorable to the continuation of democracy. However, while Lipset's interests lead him to develop modes of analysis familiar in theories of political systems and subsystems, his approach is more eclectic than that of the systems theorists. Like Lasswell and Dahl, Lipset is also concerned with who governs in democracies and other political systems. This is the meaning of his expressed interest in the factors which affect the participation of human beings in politics. To the concerns of theorists of political systems and subsystems and theorists of political influence, Lipset adds a third guiding interest. He is particularly interested in discovering the "social bases" of politics. By the social bases of politics, Lipset means the patterns of economic class and social status that condition the appearance of different political regimes. In adopting the view that political systems are conditioned by configurations of social and economic variables, Lipset places himself in the tradition of structural analysts of politics. Perhaps the most famous structural theorist of politics was Karl Marx who attempted to associate the emergence of different political regimes with systems of property ownership and production organization. Marx argued that the system of property ownership was the fundamental variable in explaining the appearance of different political regimes. Lipset adopts a more complicated view of social causation than Marx, but he still emphasizes the role of class and status variables in favoring the emergence of various political regimes. The basic question derivable from Lipset's concern with discovering the social bases of politics is, What configurations of economic class and social status favor the emergence and persistence of democratic political organization and political process in national and private governments? Thus, Lipset poses at least three basic questions. He asks the root question of theories of political systems and subsystems, How do political systems, particularly democracies, persist through stressful change? He poses the fundamental question of theories of political influence, Who governs? Finally, he asks the traditional question of theories of political structure, What social conditions favor the emergence and persistence of different political regimes?

In order to understand what Lipset means by the social bases of politics it is necessary to explore his view of the nature of political democracy. By defining democracy, we will grasp the dependent variable in Lipset's analysis, or the phenomenon that he desires to explain. The other variables in his theory will be the independent variables, or those factors that account for the emergence and persistence of democracy. These independent variables will make up the social bases of political democracy. Lipset defines democracy as it has historically appeared, rather than as it has been described by philosophers defending its desirability. Like Dahl, whose pluralist theory of democracy is meant to describe the significant variables present in the politics of New Haven and, by implication, the politics of the United States, Lipset elaborates a description of democracy applicable to practice in the Western world.

For Lipset, democracies in the West have three basic characteristics, whether they appear in national or private governments. First, democracies have a "political formula," or a "body of beliefs specifying which institutions—political parties, a free press, and so forth—are legitimate (accepted as proper by all)."[6] Here Lipset's link with theorists of the political system and subsystems is clear. A democracy is defined by specific norms and values that are widely accepted. Among these norms are respect for the kinds of freedoms listed in the American Bill of Rights and respect for majority rule. In addition to majority rule and protected rights, norms favoring discussion and compromise over violence and secession as means of resolving conflict are also necessary. By "political formula" Lipset does not mean a myth or an ideology imposed by an elite of rulers on a mass of ruled. Instead, he refers to the widely agreed upon norms and values concerning the proper limits of political decision and the processes through which decisions should be reached. Theorists of political elites like Harold Lasswell would argue that such political formulae, even in democracies, symbolize elite interests. Lipset does not make such a judgment. The second characteristic of Western democracies is the presence of one set of political leaders in public office. This is essentially an expression of the formal condition that there be a government and administration capable of devising and executing policies. Democracy, or any other political system, requires a set of roles through which values are authoritatively allocated and a set of actors who perform those roles. The third characteristic of Western democracies is the presence of one or more sets of recognized political leaders attempting to gain public office. Here Lipset states the condition of competition among parties that he believes is the essence of democratic regimes. For Lipset, the strength of a democracy can be measured by the hardiness of the opposition party or parties. Without the check supplied by a vigorous opposition, political regimes tend to become arbitrary and irresponsible. The absence of a healthy opposition in an otherwise democratic political system would likely be followed by a loss of meaningful majority rule and protected rights. The regime would become a one-party dictatorship.

Lipset argues that the absence of any of his conditions for democracy will drive a regime either to anarchy or dictatorship. In the absence of widely

[6] Lipset, *Political Man*, p. 27.

accepted norms supporting majority rule and protected rights there will be chaos bred by groups that do not support these norms. The majority will be defenseless against well-organized minorities that employ force and disruption to get their way. In the absence of a single group of officials who can make and execute relatively consistent policies, government will be controlled by shifting and irresponsible coalitions of factions. In the twentieth century Italy and France have sometimes been characterized by coalition governments composed of parties in serious conflict with one another. Under such regimes consistency of policy proved impossible and there were few authoritative allocations of value. The political system was incapable of processing many demands and was sometimes exposed to intolerable stress. Before the onset of fascism, Italy was governed by such irresponsible coalitions. Finally, as we pointed out above, in the absence of a vigorous opposition the party in power will tend to act more and more arbitrarily until meaningful majority rule is destroyed and rights go unprotected.

In his description of the characteristics of democracy, Lipset has defined a process through which values are authoritatively allocated in entire societies and partial associations. For Lipset, decisions in democracies are made by a group of officials who are accountable to an electorate. These officials face periodic competition from rival sets of leaders who challenge their policies and competence in electoral campaigns. Both governments and opposition tend to abide by majority decisions and respect fundamental civil liberties. Lipset believes that the primary social issue in the contemporary world is the battle between advocates of the kind of democracy that he defines and the proponents of one-party totalitarian dictatorships. His inquiry into the social bases of politics can be viewed as an investigation of the factors that are favorable to the success of the democratic regimes that gain his approval. He believes that political democracies only emerge in a restricted range of social conditions. This is the meaning of his basic question, What are the conditions of economic class and social status in which political systems characterized by widespread respect for majority rule and the protection of rights, a set of effective leaders and a vigorous opposition, emerge and persist? This is the basic question of a structural theorist of democracy.

The Fundamental Concepts

It is important to note that Lipset's definition of a democratic political system is more like the interpretations presented by political scientists before World War II than like those developed by current political theorists of the behavioral persuasion. The descriptions of American politics given by theorists like David Truman and Robert Dahl are far less formal and institutional than Lipset's presentation. Truman, who found interest group activities behind the behaviors in political parties, and Dahl, who found a system of dispersed inequalities among individuals and groups behind the machinery of majority rule, were pioneers in challenging the institutional approach to the study of American politics. Why should Lipset, a political sociologist, adopt an institutional definition of democratic political systems when current political theorists are no longer presenting such definitions? An answer to this question can be found by examining the differences between Lipset's basic query and the questions posed by Dahl and Truman.

Dahl, who asked who governs, was primarily concerned with bringing into question the formal institutions of government. The elite theorists had proposed that whatever formal structures of government characterized a political system an elite actually ruled. Responding to elite theory, Dahl argued and attempted to document that decisions in all political systems were not necessarily made by small ruling groups. Elite theorists had posed the question, who governs, regardless of the rules specified in formal structures of decision making. Theorists of political pluralism, like Dahl, accepted the anti-institutional assumptions and attempted to identify actual patterns of political decision making different from elite rule. While Lipset has some interest in the problems of influence, his major orientation diverges from Dahl's. Lipset is primarily concerned with identifying those social conditions that favor the appearance of a formal decision-making institution. Whoever actually rules in a democracy, the structure through which decisions are legitimated normally includes majority rule, protected rights and competitive parties. Some theorists of political influence might question the importance of investigating the social conditions favoring the emergence of a formal institution when that institution may be merely a façade masking another system of decision making. However, this objection probably does not carry much weight. If the formal rules of democratic decision making are merely a façade, they still are a façade for *something*. Thus, it would be important to investigate the social conditions favoring the appearance of the pattern of decision making behind the façade, whether it is elite rule or a system of dispersed inequalities.

David Truman, who asked how we could account for the existence of a going and generally accepted polity in a context of diverse interest groups, was calling into question the formal institutions of democracy in another way. Truman was impressed by the fact that in the American political system values were not always authoritatively allocated for society by a specific set of public officials representing a political party that had won a majority vote in an election. He found that throughout the governmental structure there were innumerable points of access through which interest groups pressed their demands. If a group was not represented by the results of an election it could attempt to have its demands satisfied in the legislature, the courts or administrative agencies. Truman was concerned with finding out how the political system persisted under the strains imposed by a multitude of interest groups seeking access to points of decision. Taking account of the sheer quantity and the controversial nature of the demands pressed by interest groups, he stated that the system persisted because of a widespread consensus on the limits of political conflict and the multi-group affiliations of many individuals. While Lipset is very interested in how democratic political systems persist, his emphasis differs from Truman's. Lipset is concerned with discovering the factors that make for the persistence of a formal system of decision making. Whatever activities interest groups undertake, political decisions in the United States are still legitimized by appeal to the formal rules of competitive party democracy. Some theorists of political systems and subsystems might claim that there are serious limitations to investigating the social conditions favoring the appearance of a specific mechanism of decision making. They might assert that systems theories, which investigate the conditions favoring the persistence of all political systems, are far more general than structural theories of democracy, or any other particular regime. Theorists of political systems and subsystems are probably correct in their claim of greater generality. The best response for structural theorists of democracy is that the investigation of a specific formal pattern of decision making, and the social conditions favoring its appearance and maintenance, will provide concepts through which a theory explaining why different structures appear can be developed. The study of the appearance and persistence of democratic institutions in nation states is nearly an example of deviant case analysis. Throughout the history of human political activity, relatively few competitive party democracies have appeared. A study of the social conditions surrounding these regimes may identify factors not found in other situations that are decisive in determining the appearance of particular decision-making structures.

In response to his basic question Lipset develops a set of interrelated explanatory concepts. Lipset claims that the primary social condition favoring the emergence and persistence of democratic institutions is a high level of economic development and a relatively even distribution of economic benefits. He asserts that economic development, "producing increased income, greater economic security, and widespread higher education, largely determines the form of the 'class struggle,' by permitting those in the lower strata to develop longer time perspectives and more complex and gradualist views of politics."[7] Further, he maintains that economic development normally produces a large middle class that rewards moderate political parties and penalizes groups that attempt to gain authoritative allocations of values through other means than majority rule bounded by protected rights. Finally, Lipset

---

[7] Lipset, *Political Man*, p. 45.

holds that in societies characterized by high levels of economic development people experience less status inferiority than they do in underdeveloped societies. By this he means that in highly developed societies production is geared to satisfy mass markets. Thus, there are no widely recognized and permanent external badges of social superiority. The rich watch the same television programs as the poor and adopt many of the same styles. In his comments on the lack of status inferiority in societies characterized by high levels of economic development Lipset may have overlooked the new divisions based on skill that Lasswell and Dahl discussed. Recurrent attacks by both left and right on intellectuals, bureaucrats and "so-called experts" belie Lipset's complacency about the relative lack of status conflicts in Western democratic societies. Contemptuous references and summary treatment to the poor and the "lower middle class" by the experts are the other side of the struggle. Regardless of significant status conflicts in contemporary Western democracies, Lipset appears to be correct that competitive party systems are associated with high levels of economic development. Increased income and economic security do allow people to broaden their time perspectives beyond short-term survival and make plans for the future. However, unless such economic security is accompanied by security from violent crime, environmental decay and nuclear war the chance for time perspectives to broaden significantly likely will be snuffed out. Further, while it is reasonable to expect that broader time perspectives will be accompanied by more complex and gradualist views of political change, the commitment to evolutionary change under a system of majority rule with protected rights is also partly dependent on a wider security than high income provides.

Lipset does not argue that a high level of economic development is the only important condition for the emergence of democratic institutions for decision making. He lists effectiveness, legitimacy and widespread crosscutting affiliations as other major factors that favor the appearance of democratic institutions. We will discuss each of these factors in turn.

Effectiveness refers to the performance of a political system, or the "extent to which the system satisfies the basic functions of government as most of the population and such powerful groups within it as big business or the armed forces see them."[8] Presumably, effectiveness is crucial for the persistence of any political system. The concept of effectiveness is similar to Easton's idea that the outputs of a political system in the form of authoritative allocations of values must satisfy a certain minimal level of demands if the system is to persist. Neither Easton nor Lipset provides a means of determining the level of effectiveness required for system maintenance. However, it is clear that some concept like effectiveness is required in theories of political systems and subsystems. It is also interesting that the concept of effectiveness allows

---

[8] Lipset, *Political Man*, p. 64.

Lipset to take account of inequalities in influence over decision making.

Legitimacy refers to the "capacity of the system to engender and maintain the belief that the existing political institutions are the most appropriate ones for the society."[9] Following Easton, legitimacy seems to be a kind of support for the political system. In this case the support would be for the regime, or the particular ways in which values are authoritatively allocated. Again, widespread belief that the existing political institutions are the most appropriate ones for the society does not seem to be a condition that only applies to the persistence of democratic political regimes. According to theorists of political systems and subsystems, the maintenance of any political system depends upon the existence of a minimum level of legitimacy. Thus far the only condition that applies specifically to the emergence and persistence of democratic political regimes is a high level of economic development.

Lipset mentions crosscutting bases of cleavage as the fourth social condition that favors the appearance and persistence of democratic political regimes. By crosscutting bases of cleavage Lipset means the widespread membership of individuals in groups that compete with one another on various issues. Individuals who are members of two or more groups that oppose one another are "cross-pressured." They are likely to withdraw from a conflict and thereby make that conflict more moderate than it would have been if they had entered the fray on one side. In advancing the idea that the widespread presence of crosscutting bases of cleavage favors political stability, Lipset is rephrasing Truman's idea that multiple memberships in competing groups minimizes the destabilizing effects of political conflict. Again, it is likely that the widespread presence of crosscutting bases of cleavage would favor the persistence of all political systems, not only democracies. It appears that Lipset's only contribution to a theory of the social conditions of democracy is his argument that a high level of economic development favors the appearance and persistence of a competitive party system under majority rule and protected rights. The other factors that he mentions, effectiveness, legitimacy and crosscutting bases of cleavage, favor the persistence of all political systems.

Imaginative Perspective

Based on his notion that stable competitive party systems are associated with high levels of economic development, Lipset claims that contemporary Western democracies are in a post-ideological phase. No longer will people engage in politics with the hope of realizing an ideal commonwealth. Democ-

---

[9] Lipset, *Political Man*, p. 64.

racy is "not only or even primarily a means through which different groups can attain their ends or seek the good society; it is the good society itself in operation."[10] The fundamental political problems of the industrial revolution have been solved. Workers have gained full citizenship and bargaining rights, conservatives have accepted the welfare state, and the left has recognized that increasing state power is dangerous to the realization of freedom. Since *Political Man* was published in 1962 many political events have occurred that cast doubt on Lipset's interpretation. The emergence of students as a politically active group, the increasing seriousness of racial tensions, the appearance of wars in former colonies and increasing awareness of environmental problems have all raised questions about the viability of competitive party democracy. At least, Lipset's idea that a large middle class and a high level of economic development will sustain representative democracy must be held up to further scrutiny.

Gabriel Almond and Sidney Verba

Gabriel Almond and Sidney Verba have each been involved in a wide range of projects in political science and political theory. Almond is best known for his work in the field of comparative government. *The Politics of Developing Areas*, which he wrote and edited with James S. Coleman, was one of the first attempts to apply theories of political systems and subsystems to the study of comparative government.[11] In *The Politics of Developing Areas*, Almond argued that there is a tendency for political systems to develop from undifferentiated structures to highly differentiated structures. For example, in some primitive societies it is impossible even to identify a set of specialized institutions that one could call a government. Religious, familial, economic and political roles overlap with one another. By contrast, in contemporary industrialized societies, not only is it possible to identify a governmental institution, but the observer is confronted with a highly specialized set of structures performing different functions such as the communications media, interest groups, political parties, legislatures, executives, administrative agencies and courts. Thus, Almond and Coleman attempted to give a temporal dimension to theories of the political system and political subsystems. Political systems tended to develop from undifferentiated and unspecialized structures performing many functions to highly differentiated and specialized structures performing a few functions or only one task. According to the

---

[10] Lipset, *Political Man*, p. 439.
[11] Gabriel Almond and James Coleman, *The Politics of Developing Areas* (Princeton: Princeton University Press, 1960).

criteria set by Almond and Coleman the United States and Great Britain were the most highly developed political systems.

Sidney Verba is best known for his work in international relations and his attempts to demonstrate the utility of social psychological research and theory for work in political science. In *Small Groups and Political Behavior,* Verba reviewed the research and theory pertaining to the study of interpersonal behavior in small groups and argued that small groups were an important aspect of many political phenomena, including socialization and decision making.[12] The interest of Almond in the properties of political systems and Verba's concern with the relationship between social psychology and politics resulted in a collaborative effort. *The Civic Culture,* published by Almond and Verba in 1963, constitutes an attempt to explore an intermediate zone between individual political decision making and the structure and function of entire political systems and political subsystems.[13] In *The Civic Culture,* Almond and Verba presented the results of a survey of political attitudes conducted in the United States, Great Britain, Germany, Italy and Mexico. They compared the configurations of political attitudes that they found in these five nations with both the political structures present in these nations and one another. Their object was to explore the kinds of political attitudes that are associated with different kinds of political systems. In our discussion of the political theories of Gabriel Almond and Sidney Verba, we will be concerned primarily with the questions posed and the concepts developed in *The Civic Culture.*

The Political Question

While Lipset was primarily interested in the social conditions that favored the emergence and persistence of democratic political institutions, Almond and Verba are most concerned with the pattern of political attitudes that support stable democratic processes. They state that they are concerned with a number of "classic themes" of political science; particularly with "what the Greeks called 'civic virtue' and its consequences for the effectiveness and stability of the democratic polity; and with the kind of community life, social organization, and upbringing of children that fosters civic virtue."[14] Thus, the basic political question of Almond and Verba is, What kind of political culture, or configuration of political attitudes, is most favorable for the persistence of democratic political systems?

---

[12] Sidney Verba, *Small Groups and Political Behavior* (Princeton: Princeton University Press, 1961).

[13] Gabriel Almond and Sidney Verba, *The Civic Culture* (Boston: Little, Brown and Company, 1965).

[14] Almond and Verba, *The Civic Culture,* p. ix.

The fundamental question of Almond and Verba can be understood best after their views of a democratic political system and political culture have been clarified. For Almond and Verba, democratic societies in the West are characterized by an "open polity" and a "civic culture." The "open polity" is a "complex infrastructure" of rules and institutions, while the "civic culture" is a set of attitudes and feelings that is associated with these institutions. When we speak of Almond's and Verba's view of a democratic political system we refer to the open polity. The conception of a democratic political system, or an open polity, that Almond and Verba present is not as formal or institutional as Lipset's conception. For the most part, it is defined by the differentiated and specialized structures that Almond and Coleman identified in *The Politics of Developing Areas.* An open polity is characterized by independent communications media that inform citizens about political affairs, interest groups through which citizens can press demands for authoritative allocations of values, political parties that compete with one another for votes and aggregate the demands of interest groups, legislatures that decide upon authoritative allocations of values, and administrative agencies that enforce these authoritative allocations. The two most important aspects of the open polity are wide opportunities for citizen participation on the demand side of the political system, and efficient and effective enforcement on the output side of the political system. Further, citizen participation in the open polity must be voluntary and the expression of demands must not be suppressed. The conception of the democratic political system presented by Almond and Coleman is close to Dahl's idea of a pluralistic democracy of dispersed inequalities and Truman's notion of a democracy characterized by interest group conflicts. Almond and Verba are particularly concerned with discovering the configuration of attitudes toward political objects that is associated and supports the open polity. They believe that the emerging non-European nations will find it easier to copy the forms of the open polity than to learn the subtle attitudes that support democratic institutions in the United States and England.

By political culture Almond and Verba mean the distribution of attitudes toward political objects that characterizes the members of a political system. Thus, Almond and Verba restrict the use of the term culture to psychological orientations toward social objects: "When we speak of the political culture of a society, we refer to the political system as internalized in the cognitions, feelings, and evaluations of its population."[15] This definition causes little difficulty because Almond and Verba use the term political system to refer to the set of roles and structures through which values are authoritatively allocated for a society. Thus, they are exploring political systems and political

---

[15] Almond and Verba, *The Civic Culture,* p. 13.

subsystems from the viewpoint of the attitudes that support or destroy structures and processes. They are much closer in approach to theorists of political systems and political subsystems, like Easton and Truman, than they are allied with theorists of political influence like Lasswell or Dahl.

Political culture has cognitive, affective and evaluative components. Individuals have knowledge of and belief about political systems, feelings about the political system and its personnel, and judgments and opinions about the political system. In addition to having orientations toward the entire political system, people have cognitive, affective and evaluative orientations toward input objects, output objects and themselves as political actors. For example, in contemporary industrialized societies people are oriented toward interest groups, political parties and conflicts over demands (input objects); laws, policies and administrative actions (output objects); and their own political decisions and participation (self as object). From the various types of orientations and the different objects of orientation, Almond and Verba derive a classification system of the types of political culture. In parochial political cultures, the frequency of orientation toward any of the four political objects (the entire system, input objects, output objects and the self as active participant) approaches zero. Parochial political cultures are usually associated with societies characterized by little structural differentiation and specialization. Where there are no distinguishable political objects, there can be no orientation toward political objects. Where there is a high frequency of orientation toward the entire system and output objects, and a low frequency of orientation toward input objects and the self as an active participant, a subject political culture exists. Subject political cultures are usually associated with centralized and authoritarian political regimes. Finally, in participant political cultures, the frequency of orientation toward all four political objects is high. Participant political cultures are associated with contemporary industrialized societies, although Almond and Verba claim that a "participation explosion" is taking place throughout the world.

The Fundamental Concepts

Almond and Verba maintain that no political culture in actual operation can be identified with any of the three pure types. All political cultures are mixtures of the various types, with some elements predominating over the others. Thus, the civic culture, which supports the open polity, or the contemporary democratic political system, is neither fully parochial, subject nor participant. Almond and Verba remark that the civic culture is not "the political culture that one finds described in civics textbooks, which prescribe the way in which citizens ought to act in a democracy."[16] The textbook

---

[16] Almond and Verba, *The Civic Culture,* p. 29.

definition of democracy stresses the requirement that citizens be fully informed and active participants on the input side of the political system. They are supposed to discuss issues, press demands and be concerned with problems that are beyond the scope of their personal lives. Like Easton, Almond and Verba fear that if this idea was carried through into practice, the political system would be placed under unbearable stress from volume and content overloads.

The civic culture contains favorable attitudes toward participation on the input side of the political system, but it also contains two other components. First, the civic culture is "an allegiant participant culture." Members of the political system are not only oriented to political input, "they also are oriented positively to the input structures and the input process."[17] In other words, members of the political system are not only favorably disposed toward political participation, they also believe that the structures of the open polity are good. In Easton's terms, there is a high level of support for the regime. In Lipset's vocabulary, the system is legitimate.

The second way in which the civic culture differs from textbook democracy is in its combination of participant political orientations with subject and parochial political orientations. There is widespread trust in other people and social participation that characterize parochial cultures. There is also respect for the acts of executive and administrative bodies that characterizes subject political cultures. The "subject and parochial orientations 'manage' or keep in place the participant political orientations."[18]

Within societies characterized by the civic culture there are individuals with relatively pure parochial, subject or participant orientations, and individuals who combine mixes of them in a somewhat contradictory fashion. The response of Almond and Verba to their basic political question—What kind of political culture, or configuration of political attitudes, is most favorable for the persistence of democratic political systems?—is "the civic culture." The civic culture is a compound of parochial, subject and participant orientations to political systems and subsystems that emphasizes favorable feelings about participation, support for political objects and widespread trust in others. This is the social-psychological condition for the persistence of representative democracy which, perhaps, supplements Lipset's structural condition of a high level of economic development.

Imaginative Perspective

Almond and Verba recognize that their description of the civic culture leaves the citizen of a democracy in a dilemma. On the one hand, the citizen is

---

[17] Almond and Verba, *The Civic Culture*, p. 30.
[18] Almond and Verba, *The Civic Culture*, p. 30.

supposed to place a high value on participation and believe that he can influence political decisions. On the other hand, the citizen is supposed to be Dahl's "civic man" who does not become a political actor unless his personal situation is directly threatened, and who gracefully accepts most of the outputs of the political system. Almond and Verba provide no way of resolving this dilemma. They believe that it is not serious as long as politics does not play an important part in the lives of most people. However, they also believe that the tension between the two horns of the dilemma is necessary to the survival of representative democracy. In a time when politics seems to be of increasing importance in the lives of many people, the paradoxes of the civic culture will be put to a severe test.

Political Theory and Political Life

6

On Classifying Political Theories

In this volume, we have examined only one short episode in the history of political thought. Before the dawn of the behavioral movement, many schools of political theory existed, each with its own distinctive questions, concepts and vision. As long as civilizations exist, political theorists will continue to create new queries, develop responses to them and articulate imaginative perspectives. Yet even within so restricted a subject as empirical theories of the behavioral persuasion, we adopted a classification system to separate different kinds of theories. This classification system was based on the different questions posed by various current political theorists. Theorists of the entire political system posed the question, How do political systems persist through stress? They were concerned with defining the integrity of political systems and discovering the most general factors that contributed to their maintenance and decay. Theorists of the political system tended to use specialized technical language borrowed from biology, engineering and cybernetics. However, this surface resemblance was not as important as the content of the question posed by all of the theorists ranged under the systems head.

Theorists of political subsystems asked the question, How do political subsystems persist through stress? Their concepts paralleled the fundamental ideas of the systems theorists, but their point of view was slightly different. They saw political affairs from the point of view of the interest groups, formal organizations and role systems within the political system, and attempted to discover how the internal structures of the units were maintained and how these units contributed to the maintenance and decay of the entire political system.

Theorists of the political system and theorists of political subsystems had in common a concern with the problem of order. Thomas Hobbes, the first modern political theorist to pose the question of order, asked, How are patterns of predictable and relatively peaceful behavior maintained in human societies? Hobbes believed that only fear of a superior force could ultimately secure order in human societies. Theorists of the political system and political subsystems disagree with Hobbes and contend that political systems and subsystems persist primarily because large numbers of people have internalized norms and values that support the sustenance of the systems.

Theorists of political influence did not pose the problem of order. They were most interested in discovering who governs, or who gets what, when and how. They concentrated on clarifying the concepts of influence and power, listing the values that one could attain through political activity and describing the methods through which these values are attained in political life. Rather than posing the problem of order, they posed what one might call the problem of power. The problem of power is also a traditional question in political theory. Plato had attempted to define a classification system for the different kinds of ruling groups that could appear in political systems, and he also described the techniques that each of these ruling groups employed. Current theorists of political influence can be divided into theorists of political elites and theorists of political pluralism, depending on the configuration of power that they find in Western democracies. Theorists of political elites believe that small ruling groups are influential in determining the outcome of a wide range of significant issues, while theorists of political pluralism hold that power is dispersed among many groups and individuals who specialize in one or two issues. Regardless of their differences in interpreting the distribution of power in Western representative democracies, theorists of political elites and theorists of political pluralism are classified together because of the question that they pose

Theorists of contemporary democracy were primarily concerned neither with the problem of order nor the problem of power. They were most interested in discovering the general social or cultural conditions favorable to the emergence and persistence of representative democratic institutions. They fixed attention on both the properties of democratic institutions and the particular social and cultural patterns that are associated with them. They had to gain a clear idea of the features of democracy so that they could isolate a set of conditions that favored its emergence and persistence. Theorists of contemporary democracy posed a particular problem of their own. They were concerned with the relationships of political activity to other modes of human activity. This question—How is the pattern of political behavior conditioned by other forms of behavior in a society?—is also a traditional problem of political theory. Montesquieu and Karl Marx attempted to relate political institutions to social and economic conditions, respectively. Plato and Auguste Comte tried to relate political institutions to social psychological and cultural conditions. Among theorists of contemporary democracy there are also two approaches. Some theorists attempt to relate the emergence and persistence of Western representative democracy to levels of economic development. Other theorists try to relate the maintenance of contemporary democracies to a complex of attitudes that is widespread in the population. Theorists of contemporary democracy who take a sociological approach and those who take a social psychological and cultural approach are listed under the same heading because their essential question is, What are the relationships between political activity and other modes of human activity?

Classifying political theories by the questions that political theorists pose has the advantage of preserving the intentions of the theorists under examination. One does not impose categories upon the political theories that their creators would not understand. Further, one does not embark on a search for hidden meanings behind the political theories or the efforts of their creators. When one classifies political theories by their basic questions he is treating them as serious intellectual endeavors. He is treating them with respect because he is studying them on their own terms and is not attempting to reduce them to another language or another set of problems. However, while it is worthwhile to treat theorists and their work with respect, as long as they deserve it, there are times when it is also useful to impose alien categories on political theories. Thus, there are many alternative ways of classifying political theories.

When one departs from the questions posed as his primary basis of classifying political theories, he develops a classification system in response to a specific question of his own. Perhaps the crudest way of categorizing political theories is by ordering them in a temporal sequence. When political theories are classified according to whether they were written in the eighteenth, nineteenth or twentieth centuries, the system of categories has been developed in response to the question, How do political theories differ over time? Similar to classification in temporal sequence is categorization by space. Political theories are often classified according to whether they appeared in Europe, Asia or the United States. Here, the question is, How do political theories differ over space? or, How do political theories differ over culture area? The classification of political theories according to when and where they were written is characteristic of many textbooks and university courses in political theory. It provides a relatively simple way of classifying works of thought because, ultimately, human societies are extended frameworks of space and time relations. However, these category schemes have the limitation that the questions—How do political theories differ over time? and, How do political theories differ over space?—are not primarily questions about political life. They are questions about political theories themselves. Thus, while political theories are one step removed from political affairs because they are generalizations about politics, classifications of political theories by space and time are at least two steps removed from politics.

Other ways of classifying political theories are far more sophisticated than categorization by time or space. Sometimes political theories are classified under the categories of another political theory. Thus, Easton might classify political theories as "theories of inputs," "theories of outputs" and "theories of feedback." If he undertook this effort he would be claiming that some political theorists stress the input side of the political system, others stress the output side of the political system and still others emphasize the feedback loop. Perhaps Easton might even say that he has developed a theory of feedback. The classification of political theories under the categories of another political theory imposes the emphases of one political theorist on others. There is an inevitable distortion of the authors categorized and usually the theory that is being used as the base of classification is illuminated more than the theories being categorized. However, despite the distortion, the classification of political theories under the categories of another political theory is often very useful and informative. First, it may illumine aspects of the classified political theories that have been virtually ignored in the past. These new insights can be the sources of advance in political theory. Thus, classifying Dahl's theory under Easton's categories as a theory of input places Dahl's work in a wider perspective and shows its limitations as a complete theory of political activity. Second, this classification may help place the theory being used as a base of classification in a historical tradition. The activity of showing that one's theory is the culmination of a long historical progression is perhaps essential for the maintenance of cultural continuity. Thus, Truman and Dahl give historical respectability to their works by arguing that James Madison, Karl Marx and Max Weber were early theorists of political groups. Third, this classification often allows a political theorist to clearly define the differences between his theory and the efforts of the past. Such classification systems are frequently used as tools for criticizing other political theories. Thus, Easton has criticized other political theorists for lack of comprehensive scope because they presented only theories of specific regimes. Finally, the classification of political theories under the category system of another political theory can aid in the synthesis of concepts from a wide range of political theories. By such synthesizing activity the theorist can bring much of the knowledge of the past to bear on the solution of his particular question. Concepts that were employed in response to a wide variety of queries can be rearranged to solve new problems. Perhaps the most conspicuous use of classification for the purposes of synthesis that has been discussed in this study is Lasswell's revaluation of past political knowledge in terms of its bearing on the ways in which elites seek and maintain influence. No significant political theorist begins his work with a blank slate for a mind. Originality in political theory is the result of extensive and deep knowledge of the traditions of political theorizing.

Classification of political theories under the category system of another political theory is usually more of an aid in understanding the base of classification than it is a help in comprehending the classified theories. Similar to this is classification by units of analysis or key concepts. In classification by units of analysis or key concepts, the theorist develops a list of fundamental concepts describing political activity. After he has compiled his list, he classifies political theories in accordance with the concept that he believes they emphasize. Such classification systems frequently distort the political theories under examination. Essentially, they are proto-theories of political activity and they may aid the theorist who develops them in advancing his own theoretical system. Further, if the theorist is a sensitive observer, he may develop a list of concepts that comes close to being an adequate categorization of the theories under study.

Very much like classification by a list of units of analysis or fundamental concepts is classification by possible answers to key questions. For example, Dahl classified political theorists by their answer to the question, Who governs? Classical democratic theorists claim that political parties govern, interest group theorists hold that interest groups govern, theorists of political elites maintain that elites govern, mass society theorists claim that the masses and demagogues govern, and theorists of political pluralism argue that dispersed groups and clusters of individuals rule. While all of the theorists examined in this volume could be classified according to Dahl's category system, such a classification would deprive the student of understanding the central significance of many of them. However, we saw how valuable Dahl's classification system was for illuminating his own theory of dispersed inequalities. He was able to place his own thoughts in a historical perspective, use concepts developed by others for advancing his own theoretical propositions and contrast his results with the conclusions of others.

Finally, political theories can be classified according to the degree to which they approach the standard of an ideal political theory. While this way of classifying theories illuminates the logical structure of scientific theory, it does little else. Classification systems of political theories can be valuable for a wide variety of purposes. It is most important to keep in mind the specific problem that these categories are meant to resolve.

Some Uses of Political Theory

Most people do not pose the questions asked by current political theorists of the behavioral persuasion. In everyday political life the questions—How do political systems persist through change? How do political subsystems persist under stress? Who gets what, when and how? What are the socioeconomic and social psychological conditions for the emergence and persistence of democracy?—are concealed beneath debates about whether particular groups are fomenting violent revolution, whether certain groups are aware of the proper function of an organization, whether a particular person will succeed in getting his way in a certain conflict, or whether a new government program will influence more people to accept the "system." Are the political theories discussed in this book useful in interpreting the political events that take place day by day? The answer that has been implied in the preceding pages is affirmative. Current political theories are useful in the interpretation of ordinary political life because they provide alternative perspectives through which to view the political world. The individual can enhance his understanding of the political situations that he reads about and the political activities in which he engages by adopting different viewpoints. By adopting different perspectives the individual clarifies, generalizes and relativizes his predicament. He also discovers new possibilities for action and, perhaps, new values. All of these uses of political theory are important to the attainment of the good life.

It is reasonable to say that everyone who reads this book is oriented in some way toward political objects. Following Almond and Verba, people will be oriented toward the entire political system, input objects like interest groups, action groups and political parties, output objects like laws and regulations, and themselves as participants in political activity. These orientations will include assumptions about the nature of the political objects, feelings about them, and judgments about their rightness and wrongness. Further, people will either have allegiance to political objects, feel apathetic about them or be alienated from them. In the case of allegiance, people will have assumptions about the nature of political objects, and have positive feelings for, and evaluations of, them. In the case of apathy, people will have assumptions about the nature of political objects, and be otherwise indifferent toward them. In the case of alienation, people will have assumptions about the nature of political objects, and have negative feelings for, and evaluations of, them. Thus, whether the person supports political objects, is indifferent toward them, or repudiates them, he will have assumptions about their nature. Normally, these assumptions are concealed. The person is not fully aware of them and he is not cognizant of their implications. However, these assumptions about political objects constitute a personal political theory. They include the questions that the person usually asks about political life, the concepts that he employs to respond to these questions, and the perspective through which he views political events. All of these aspects of the personal political theory help condition the individual's political activity.

The study of explicit and fully developed political theories helps the individual clarify his own working assumptions about political objects. By seeing where he agrees and disagrees with a political theorist, the person becomes more aware of his own view of politics. By adopting the perspective implied in a fully developed political theory, the individual can note the differences between it and his everyday view of political life. After clarifying his personal political theory by bringing it into consciousness through comparison with another view of political affairs, the individual has the means to alter his assumptions about political objects and exert some conscious control over his public actions. The clarification of one's personal political theory is the most important function that explicit political theory performs for the acting individual. When people say that they have gained "insight" or have been "stimulated," political theory has performed its clarifying function.

One of the reasons most individuals have concealed assumptions about political objects is that they have particularized their relationships to political objects. They are not oriented toward the political system in general as much as they are involved with a succession of specific issues and particular people. They may articulate vague, general and contradictory statements about life, religion and politics. However, these assertions usually have little to do with the working assumptions that guide their actions. These working assumptions are rules of conduct geared to specific situations.

One of the most important features of political theory is its emphasis on general and abstract concepts that transcend particular situations. When one adopts the viewpoint of theorists of the political system, he finds himself in the situation of pressing demands or providing supports to a structured process for authoritatively allocating values for a society. When one adopts the perspective of theorists of political influence, he finds himself using standardized means to attain socially available values. Whatever perspective he adopts, the individual will have two experiences. First, he will have the experience of realizing that he is doing something that many people have done before him. He will understand that much of his own predicament is not personal and unique, but part of the human condition. Just this knowledge may provide more peace of mind and confidence in action. Second, he will have some appreciation of the wider consequences of his action. From the viewpoint of systems theory, he will see his action as part of a much wider system of behavior. From the perspective of theories of political influence, he will judge the consequences of his action in terms of probable changes in power relationships. Through an understanding of the consequences of his actions, the person will have the means to become a more responsible political actor.

Generalizing one's situation beyond particular political relationships has some unintended consequences. Through the processes of both clarification and generalization the person is enabled to attain a greater appreciation of others. The clarification that comes from contrasting one's personal political theory with a political theory worked out by another individual does not only give the person a fuller understanding of his own perspective. It also allows him to experience the perspective of another person. Whether or not he accepts that perspective, he will be able to appreciate the reasons why people who adopt it engage in certain kinds of political discourse and action. This knowledge may not lead to tolerance, sympathy or moderation; in fact, it may provide more effective means of manipulating other people. It will provide an understanding of others that can be used to attain a wide variety of ends. While clarification allows one to appreciate others by contrasting their perspectives with one's own, generalization furthers understanding of others by pointing up one's likeness to them. Just knowledge of the fact that all people share certain orientations to political objects allows us to understand the political discourse and activity of others. Similarly, awareness of the notion that all bureaucratic organizations function to limit the decisional premises of actors creates a bond with all people involved in such organizations. Again, such knowledge of likeness may not result in cooperation or sympathy. It can be used just as effectively as knowledge of difference for exploiting and manipulating others. However, to exploit others through knowledge of a common human condition betrays a profound disrespect for oneself. It is just such exploitation that forms the background of the nightmare of a civil war fought over status and Lasswell's frightful vision of a garrison state ordered like a military barracks.

Clarification and generalization of one's personal political theory and predicament may result in relativization of that predicament. When one is able to contrast his perspective with another person's viewpoint he becomes aware that his vision of politics is not the only possible perspective. He may become capable of interpreting political objects through a wide variety of perspectives. This can be an exciting and an enriching experience. The ability to relativize can lead to a wide range of results. First, the person may compare his perspective to the other's vision and claim superiority for his own view. He will comprehend the other's assumptions, but he will believe that they are incorrect. Second, the person may compare his perspective to the other's vision and claim that both views are correct on the ground that each individual has a right to his own political perspective. People choose what is right for them. Third, the person may compare his perspective to the other's vision and claim that both views are incorrect. He will argue that differences among perspectives are evidence that all perspectives must be abandoned as false. Such a person may despair over the loss of a conceptual anchor and yet be unable to adopt any perspective. Fourth, the person may compare his perspective to the other's vision and immediately adopt the other's view as superior. Each of these responses to relativization is unwise. All of them show a preoccupation with the differences between perspectives over their similarities. In the first and fourth cases the person overvalues adherence to a rigid perspective and fails to understand how his experience can be enhanced by the selective creation of a new perspective. In the second and third cases the person undervalues adherence to any perspective and misses much of the significance of ordered experience. When relativization is abandoned for adherence to a rigid perspective, fanaticism results. When relativization is embraced as a final experience, trivialization of experience results. While relativization can have disastrous consequences for the good life, it can also be an important means to human fulfillment. How is this possible?

Clarification, generalization and relativization open up new possibilities for thought and action. People who ask new questions about political objects or develop new systems of concepts in response to traditional questions, provide new ways of orienting the individual toward political life. Their concepts illumine new areas of human activity and show one aspects of human existence that he may have neglected. A new vision may convince one to act differently in public life. The appropriate way to respond to relativization is to be receptive to new perspectives. This does not mean that one must continuously abandon his view of the political world. Instead, it means that one should consciously search for new and valuable experiences that he can integrate with the perspective that he holds. Sometimes a new experience will be so deep and significant that the person will have to alter a great deal of his vision. Unfortunately, such experiences are rare. When they come, they are unmistakable. As the person expands his experience and understanding, he should keep in mind that it is relative to a human condition that all people share. The explicit specification of this human condition is at best incomplete. The task of defining it is the work of those disciplines that discuss the possibilities of human beings. All people who can clarify, generalize and relativize can contribute to these disciplines.

Theories of political systems, political subsystems, political influence and contemporary democracy all have perspectives to contribute to the quest for valuable human possibilities. The perspective of theories of political systems and political subsystems is particularly illuminating in a world marked by continuous crisis. The many crises in the twentieth century call into question the strength of political systems. Posing the problem of order and responding to it is a way of contributing to a search for order in a world marked by much chaos. The perspective of theories of political influence illumines the conflicts that underly contemporary crisis situations. They explore the patterns of domination and revolution, and allow the person to situate himself within the conflicts. The perspective of theories of contemporary democracy leads one to understand the historical specificity of particular political systems. Knowledge of some of the conditions that favor the persistence of representative democracies is also knowledge of the history and culture in which one exists. With such knowledge, one may act with reference to a tradition. Whether he embraces, repudiates or revises and reconceives that tradition, he will be aware of the historical dimensions of what he is thinking and doing. These are, perhaps, the most significant contributions of current political theories.